ALIEN INT

One Man's Account ⸱   ⸱⸱ Days
When Reality Changed for Him

By Mike Oram and Fran Pickering

Star Hill Publishing
Lake District. UK

Published by Star Hill Publishing 2011
www.starhillpublishing.co.uk

ISBN: 978-1-907710-07-0

Contents

Preface

This is the true story of one man's adventure on Earth and beyond. He is not alone in his claims to have met with beings from beyond our Time and Space. We live in an age when many, many ordinary people are making extraordinary claims: claims of seeing and interacting with beings not from Earth; claims that not only are we not alone on our journey through space but that our spaceship Earth is indeed being visited by other craft and other creatures, who are making themselves known in many ways.

We humans are as different inside our minds as we are in our physical bodies and many tales of alien encounters may well originate in imagination or delusion - but what if some people tell such bizarre stories because they are recounting what really happened to them? What if many people the world over, from differing cultures with diverse educational abilities and professions, are telling similar tales because these things are true? Truth is, in the end, they say, stranger than fiction.

Here, for you to believe or disbelieve, is one man's tale of terror and trauma, contact and communication with visiting neighbours from our own galaxy. Travellers on the same journey as us. So, I ask you to do three things:

1. Suspend disbelief until you come to the end of the story.

2. Remember that this adventure happened in 1964, long before the 'X-Files' hit our screens, before mainstream UFO magazines hit the bookstands and images of little grey aliens were commonplace. Long before the UK began to store the world's radioactive waste or the mass media talked of holes in the ozone layer; both of which were predicted by George's alien visitors.

3. Don't stop here. Read more. There are more than enough books, magazines and web sites to choose from. Open your mind and consider the possibility that we truly are not alone. If you discount 99% of the mass of taped interviews, video evidence, books, reports, medical evidence and artefacts pertaining to the UFO enigma, that still leaves a huge, world-wide body of claims that are hard to discount. Either we have a collective, planet-wide illusion in operation or something real is happening to real people in real time. Think about it. The most precious gift you have is your mind. Like all gifts, it is useless until it is opened.

Foreword

I spent six weeks interviewing this man whom we shall call George. He wishes to remain anonymous and you will understand why when you read his story.

George spent three separate days on board a Flying Saucer, as they were then called, the last two visits by prior arrangement. The whole story of the strangest time of his life is quite amazing.

George's second and third encounters were at a gravel pit at East Cranmore, near Shepton Mallet, close by the area in which he lived for six years up to the date when his adventure begins. What I found very interesting was that between the years 1976 and 1983 I lived in Warminster, about 17 miles from Shepton Mallet, and those gravel pits were often the location of strange events. I remember on one occasion, a night worker refused to work alone because lights were often seen moving around the quarry bottom and the general area.

This book is written in the form of an interview between myself and George, because this is the way it happened when George told his story. In the majority of instances, the words used to describe events are George's own words.

The full story was not told to us until twenty-eight years after it had happened and, as you read the incredible events and the effect they had on George, you will, perhaps, understand why he felt unable to both recount what took place and fully face how these three days so dramatically changed his life. You will also understand why, in the end, he had to pass on the message given to him by his friend from the stars because what he was told affects each and every one of us.

Mike Oram

Chapter 1
The Adventure Begins

During December 1964, an ordinary family man went for a stroll one evening and walked into a situation that changed his life forever. As a result of what happened to him and the effect it had on him, he left his home and family and wandered the globe, seeking always to escape the inescapable[1.]

His encounter with some of our near neighbours in the galaxy happened during the run-up to what became known as 'The Warminster Flap'. From Christmas Day 1964 until the late 1970s, Warminster was the geographical centre of an area of an unprecedented spate of unusual happenings. Not only were many unidentified craft seen in the skies but many people experienced other phenomena, such as balls of light moving along the High Street or strange humming sounds that could not be traced and sounds as of someone on a house roof, rattling the tiles, but then no one would be there when householders rushed out to investigate.

As time passed and we entered the 1990s, the pressure of the messages given to him by the aliens, many of them relating to the end of the century and the early part of the next, wore on George and he made attempts to pass on what he had been told. He wrote to the Ministry of Defence, the Air Ministry, the then Prime Minister, Margaret Thatcher and an organisation called 'Justice'. None acknowledged his letters. He then contacted Jenny Randles, a well-known UFO investigator and TV personality who, in turn, passed his letter on to the Northern UFO Investigation Group because George was at that time living in the Lancashire area. I was at that time an investigator for the group. What follows is George's story, as he told it over a period of six weeks.

George Tells Us His Story.

Mike: *George, you say this happened in 1964. Can you be a little more precise?*

George: It was December; the beginning of December. I don't have an exact date but I remember it very well. I went to see my daughter in Frome. After I left her, I went for a walk along the edge of the woods at Longleat. The outskirts of Longleat are just at the back of the mount in Frome.

It was a clear, moonlit night. I was walking along happily when suddenly I was grabbed! I was scared out of my wits. There were three 'creatures' tugging at me and I thought at first it must be some of the animals from Longleat which had escaped. I hit out a couple of times and it was just like hitting something solid. In the struggle I got a few scratches and my anorak was torn but, in the end, they overpowered me, with enormous strength. I was terrified and being so close to them the smell was awful, almost worse than the terror. I noticed that they were wearing what looked like 'bib and brace' overalls. It was dark remember, but they looked like grey overalls and the creatures had thick fur.

What was the smell like?

It was very rank, very sour. I passed out, by the way, during this period. I think what made me pass out was that I looked straight into one of their faces. They were only small, about three feet six inches or four feet high (105 - 120 cms) and their eyes were like glowing red coals and I passed out.

When I came to, I was inside what, at first, I took to be a room and there were two people who looked human; two males who looked human. I remember exactly what they were wearing: a one-piece, matt-grey outfit including the feet. It seemed to be all in one piece.

Would this be similar to flight clothing?

Yes, but tight fitting. I was sitting on a chair. This chair was rather surprising when I came to my senses; I stood up and I balanced myself against the chair and it was just a solid chair but when I sat down it seemed to mould to my shape.

At that point another person came into the room and it was obviously a woman. I didn't even notice what they looked like. I just thought; "Thank God! They're human!"

Right away one man spoke to me - I'm going to say this now so that I won't have to say it later - when I say they 'spoke' to me, remember that I was trained in the RAF to be observant and I noticed that neither the face nor the lips moved because they had no lips, just a slit, but he spoke to me in perfect English, no accent.

Was this an audible sound or were you hearing it in your head?

I don't know. It sounded as though they were speaking to me but I can't say whether they were or not. He apologised for the behaviour of the 'creatures' and they told me I had been hurt because these creatures had not obeyed their orders. They had taken me to this craft.

At this point I must go back to just before I went into the craft, if that's what it was. I remember coming to momentarily when I was being dragged by the arms. I saw nothing: no craft, no house, nothing. I was taken into blinding light - blinding. Then everything became subdued and I passed out again. When I came to, I was on the chair. I tried to get up. It looked like a metal chair yet when I sat back, I seemed to fit into it.

This person said to me: "We must apologise. These are our servants. They are animals, trained animals, exactly as you have cats, dogs, etc., in your own world. These are ours and they have disobeyed orders!"

The creatures were also in the room, standing by the three of them.

"We are sorry, but you are going to have after-effects from this; you were not meant to be taken aboard the craft."

Apparently, I should not have been aboard straight away; they had only just arrived there. Nobody should have gone near the craft for a period, I don't know how long. It caused me an awful lot of scarring and blisters. I still have a lot of the marks to this day.

At this point I asked for a drink of water. They brought me a beaker. It looked like an ordinary glass beaker you could see through, with green stuff in it. I raised it and looked at it. It was like jelly which had not set. He watched me and he must have read my thoughts because he took it from me and poured some out and then handed it back. So, I drank because my throat was so dry. It was very refreshing; it was very sweet. As I say, he spoke to me but I could see no movement of the facial muscles. As he was speaking this lady came in and she started talking to these three creatures. When I heard talking it was similar to castanets clicking, clicking. He explained to me that they were being reprimanded for disobeying orders. Then he told me that I had nothing to fear; that after a time of talking I would be free to go.

"The only thing we ask is that you tell no one about this because it would create a dangerous situation for yourself, not for us," he said.

Did he say in what way?

No, not at that point. There was seven and a half hours conversation over three days. For some reason I was completely at ease by this time. The room was bare. The chairs came from the wall.

What shape was the room?

5

Circular. There was absolutely no colour. It was lit - I can't explain it; it seemed like a violet light, very light violet, but I couldn't see where the light was coming from. He said that this would be the first of many meetings and he asked me if I would think about going back with them, as many others had done before. He explained to me that there are many people from this planet living with them. Some have come back under assumed identities and they are working for them.

It was at this point that I asked him why they were going back under other identities.

He said; "Because we are not the only visitors that you have. Many of my friends come, but there are two other forms of life that come, not with good intentions; to create trouble, to create havoc. They've done it for many, many years and they have been highly successful."

I said, "Well, where do you come from?" He laughed. It was a very unusual laugh, a pleasant laugh, like tinkling glass. By this time, I was perfectly at ease with them. I thought that if they were going to harm me, they would have done it by now.

They told me they were going to treat me for the injuries I had received and they asked me to take my clothes off. I looked at this obvious female and the two men laughed. She went out. I got undressed because I was all torn. One went over and touched something and a table came out of the floor. Then he opened it up and asked me to get on it. I got on it and lay down and he raised it higher. The woman came back in and they rubbed what looked like cream all over me. He said that it wouldn't stop the damage but it would help me.

Then he explained to me how I got injured: these creatures had not obeyed orders; they were to keep me away from the craft for half an hour. The craft had just arrived.

"We dropped our servants off, then came back when we found they had caught someone."

I said, "So you actually grab people?"

He said, "No! I told you, they disobeyed orders. They were supposed to find somebody, notify us, then we would come and approach them, but they took the law into their own hands."

"So, they can think?"

"Oh yes, of course they can think! They've been programmed to do what they are told, not think for themselves."

"Why aren't they doing anything now?"

"When they are in the craft, they do nothing. We are in charge of the craft."

"How many are you?"

"Just the three of us. If you get your clothes back on, we'll continue."

So, I put back on most of my clothes, except the jacket, and went and sat in the chair. The table was put back into the floor. I could see the join where it fitted. Then he explained that I was in the bottom section of the craft.

"So, you've got two sections?"

"Yes."

Right in the centre there was a huge pillar. I asked: "Can I see the controls? I used to fly when I was young."

He said, "When you were young?" He laughed. "How long ago was this?"

"I don't suppose you know, but we had a war."

"Oh yes, we know."
"Well, we called it the Second World War."

He said, "Yes, in the year 1939."

I said, "Yes."

"We watched it. We watched everything. We tried to help, but people couldn't be helped. That war was preventable, as everything is preventable, but there are forces at work to make sure these things are not prevented. Many things are going to happen in your world, many things, leading to the year 1999. In the middle of that year, in the seventh month you will start to have catastrophes, loss of life, very much so. Most of it will be natural calamity but some of it will be engineered by another life form. Would you like to see some of the evidence we have to prove that your own people are destroying yourselves?"[2]

I said, "Yes."

"It's quite simple. Just watch the wall." It came up as a picture, about the width of that wall (pointing to the wall of the interview room, which was about 9 metres wide and 2.5 metres high) and about half the height. It was three-dimensional; you could virtually see into it. He showed me what looked like huge caverns, huge caves. He said that was the inside of our planet which was being emptied, taken out.

I asked, "What do you mean 'taken out'?"

"All the natural resources of your planet are being taken out, so therefore the strength of your world is not what it should be. Viewing your world from our world, it is not round, as you fondly imagine. You'll find it is pear-shaped. The gravitational pull is pulling the weak section and eventually it will tear it away from the Earth."

By this time, I was quite alarmed. I said, "I can't understand. What is that?"

He said, "At one time your earth was full of natural resources: gas, oil, as you call it. It was being taken out in very large quantities. You have taken it out. Try to understand that if you have a box of items and you start taking them out, the box will eventually be empty, won't it?"

"Yes."

"I think a better way to say it is as a bag: pull it, take it out and the bag collapses."

"Yes, I can understand that."

"That's the interior of your world. Now the outside of your world; you have been taking away everything that breathes in the poisons that you have in your atmosphere and that breathes out the oxygen that you breathe. Again, you have been destroying that, so therefore your planet is fast becoming derelict."

I asked, "Where did you learn English?"

"We've been able to speak your language for many, many years; thousands of your years. We speak all languages. We have listened to your broadcasts; we've watched your television. We've had our people on your world for thousands of years; thousands of years."

Then they asked me to rest for a few minutes and left the room. The three creatures went out with them. The other person came back in by himself. He pulled a chair out and sat down. He didn't speak for ten or fifteen minutes. An interesting point arose then because I looked at my watch; it had stopped half an hour beforehand. It was a wind-up watch. I wound it up tight; it still wasn't going. He looked across at me and I said, "It's not working." He didn't answer me.

The other man came in and said, "It's no use speaking to him, he doesn't understand English. Some of us understand; others understand what you call Italian, Spanish, any language. We have people all over your world who speak the languages and understand the ways."

"And the lady?"

"She understands every word."

At that point this man made a clickety noise; the other answered him, then he got up and went out. The man said, "I think perhaps you've had enough, but can I ask you something?"

"Of course."

"Would you like to meet us again?"
"Yes."

He said, "Would you not say anything to anyone about this meeting?"

I said, "No, I dare not tell anyone, they'd laugh their bloody heads off at me!"

He said, "That's part of our protection. We don't want to come to this area again, it is much too near habitations."

The pub was only a couple of hundred yards away. Nobody saw anything from the pub, or heard anything.

He said, "Is there any place that you can think of where we could meet?"

I was wracking my brains trying to think of where I could ask a flying saucer to meet me! I then suggested the road to Shepton Mallet, and I said, "Oh, there is a big quarry on the right-hand side of the road when you go outside Frome. Now, at the back of that it's very quiet."

He just looked at me and smiled, he actually smiled. He said, "Yes, we do know that area rather well! We'll make it that spot - and don't worry, we'll find you! You tell us what day you'll be there. Shall we make it 8 p.m. your time?"

I said, "Yes."

"All right. You know that the quarry is open, don't you?"

"Yes."

"Well, just walk into the quarry and we'll find you. Shall we say next Thursday evening?"

I said, "Yes, all right."

I remember that well; it was a Thursday and the final meeting was the Saturday after.
They took me out of this craft. He said, "I will walk with you a short distance. Do not look round please."

11

He walked with me a good fifty yards. He stopped and said, "Now you can keep walking but, please, for your own sake, do not turn round until you've walked at least the same distance."

So, I did this, keeping my ears open. As you know, in that area it is dead quiet. I heard nothing, absolutely nothing, but when I turned round there was nothing there. They had gone.

Mike: *That was when you had walked on another fifty yards?*
Yes. I counted fifty paces. I remember doing that. You may wonder how I have such recall but, as I told you, I spent a long while training in the RAF so I was trained to remember and observe; that never leaves you. I turned round and walked back. To this day I will never know why I walked back. I walked to the spot where I had come out of whatever it was and the air was warm. It was a winter's night, remember, but the air was warm in that spot.

I started to walk back home[3] and on the way home I thought, "How do I explain this, with everything torn?" These things, the creatures, had three 'talons' and had ripped me all down, my clothes, everything, deep into the chest and on my face. I thought they were treating me for the burns on the craft when they put that cream on me, but they must have given me something to put me to sleep. They must have done.

The next thing I remember is being inside a car. I was found lying at the side of the road by a police car. The police were amazed that I was still warm despite the winter weather. It looked as though I had just fallen there. When they took me to the Frome hospital the doctors came into the ambulance and decided they could not treat me there. With a police escort, they raced me to Bath.

Three or four days afterwards I signed myself out and went home.

My wounds healed up within a few days. My doctor had never seen anything like it in his life. The burns had virtually healed in four days. I went back to the hospital. The lady doctor examined me, then looked again. She went and brought another doctor; he looked and couldn't believe it. He said he had never seen wounds heal up so fast; they had virtually disappeared. (*Mike's note: George still had small scars, at least on his arms, when he came to see us in 1992*)

Anyway, when I signed myself out and went home, I bundled up the clothes that were torn and took them outside and put them in the bin. I went into the back garden and opened the waste bin. I shut the bin, went back in and my wife said, "What are you doing home? The hospital did not tell me they were discharging you! What's the matter with you?"

I said, "If I tell you, you'll get me certified!"

"No, seriously, what the hell is wrong with you?"

I just said, "No, it's all right love." And that was the start of our rot, I now believe. She couldn't understand why I wouldn't talk about anything.

The doctor said, "I think you did have an unusual experience. You were rambling about something from outer space."

But some of those people contacted the press and there were articles in the local papers. (*Editor's Note: At that time local papers in the areas of Bath, Frome, Warminster, Shepton Mallet, ran items on such topics because of the Warminster Flap and general activity in the region*)

Mike: *Could you give me a description of these creatures?*

They were about four feet tall; I would say. They had very, very thick hair, which almost felt like wire.

What colour was the hair?

Jet black. The eyes were very red and very small. The ears were long, very obvious, pointed. The arms almost touched the ground, almost but not quite, but they only had three fingers, that I remember well. I couldn't see their feet; they were covered by the overall. The arms were bare. The first time I saw them clearly, I thought they were robots. When I hit out at them it was like hitting a stone wall or something solid, there was no give of any kind. As a matter of fact, I had the marks for weeks.

Were their eyes shaped like ours?

No, they were just like marbles; they were round. The face was completely covered in hair. The nose was virtually non-existent, just two openings. A very big mouth. I didn't see any teeth. They had enormous strength.

Did they make any noise, any sort of sound?

Yes, like a grunt. When I started struggling, they grunted away like mad. I don't think I was panicky, but I was scared. I thought they had escaped from Longleat.

Not a lot happened that first time, except to allay my fears. He did say to me at one point, just before I left, that it wouldn't be advisable to talk to anyone about this and that, if I did try, I might have great difficulty remembering. It wasn't a threat; it was said in a very friendly way. As a matter of fact, when he walked with me the fifty paces, he actually held my arm, not in a grip, just held it in a friendly way. When I put my hand out to shake his, he did the same.

Mike: *Did it feel warm?*

I don't remember that. It was just like shaking anyone's hand. Oh - one thing I did notice - no fingernails!

No fingernails?

No!

Could you describe these people for us?

Oh yes. They were human. Slightly taller than me. I'm 5'7". They would be about 6'. The obvious female was my size, because when she stood beside me, I was looking into her eyes. Their eyes were lovely; almond-shaped and bluish.

Were they the same size as our eyes?

No, much larger. They went round the side of the head. At one point he did tell me that they could see sideways. They were very gentle, very thoughtful, and gave you the feeling very quickly of being at ease; within minutes I was at ease with them.

Was their skin the same colour as ours?

It was pale skin; very, very clear, almost transparent. They are very good looking by the way, except for the lips.

The lips?

The lips were slits. They looked as though they had lips but they were sealed. There was a light touch of red. On one of the visits, I was told that some of them had undergone, as he called it, 'bodily restructuring' and were actually living on this world. He could only stay in our atmosphere for twenty-four hours at a time but if they have restructuring, they can live here. He said it's very simple but he chose not to.

Did you see anything of their ears?

Let me leave that until we get onto the second and third visit because it will spoil the continuity of it, because the first time they were completely covered with their uniform, it was all one piece. They had an emblem on the chest, just exactly where we wear ours. It was just like condensed fork-lightning. It was quite a thick line and was inside a circle. It seemed to be part of the uniform. The three of them wore that but there were no distinguishing marks like rank, there was nothing; they all looked alike. The colour was matt grey, like a metallic grey; it was brighter than the creatures' uniforms. It was like silver but without the shine. It must have been very pliable because it was so tight-fitting.

No zips, buttons?

I didn't see any. How they got it on I don't know; it was so tight.

I spotted the woman. He said something to her in the 'click click' language and she left the room. He turned to me and said, "We have bred from humans. Our women have bred, which means we have been able to send people to your planet who are exactly the same without bodily restructuring. They are born as you are; not all, but most. Our womenfolk who travel in our craft are prepared to breed with a human male."

"What about their husbands?"

He said their attitude, as with all these things (as he put it), was a great deal more civilised than our attitudes are on this world. "It is only a small part of a life of a man and woman."

The other thing that I missed out, which was regarding these pictures that they showed, was that it was just like looking right into the picture.

These were vast caverns. It was at this point he told me that we have not even begun to properly explore our own planet yet but we are trying to explore others.

He told me they have bases on the earth and on the moon. I asked him how long it took them to get here. He said, "That depends on whether we come from our home planet or one of our bases on the moon. Your people know about these bases but they also know that there is nothing they can do about it except cause lots of trouble for themselves. We are here to help."

Mike: *Did he mention how the breeding took place?*
Yes, as a matter of fact, he did. I tried to say it nicely a minute or two ago, but I was offered her company. Because of the way I was mixed up I automatically said 'no' and he didn't push the point but it was repeated on the second and third visit; an opportunity which I didn't accept, don't ask me why, because she was obviously a woman, with a perfect figure, but I turned it down. Whether I was scared, uncertain, or what, I don't know, but I did turn it down. They were very kind and courteous; they didn't push me. There is no way I could say to anyone "If you meet one of these people, run!" I would say, "Stand your ground and offer your hand, they will take it."

Mike: *Did you ever see what his craft looked like?*

Oh yes. The second time. It had three balls underneath. (Here George was shown a picture of a craft often sighted in the 60s). That's it! It's quite a good likeness, except that the centre piece here was slightly more pronounced, because that was the second part. The control is in the top section which I was in. It's in three sections outside: there's an inner, a centre and an outer and two of them revolve in opposite directions, but the centre stays still.

Did he say what powered it?

When I asked him that he pointed at the centre pillar and he laughed again and said, "That is propulsion."

I said, "How does it work?" He just looked at me and never answered. He smiled and never answered me.

At one point I asked him about the 'Warminster flap' and mentioned three huge circles of flattened crop that had appeared in fields. I asked if they had been made by craft. He said their craft do not leave any trace at all but that there had been occasions when scout craft, which are smaller, have landed in fields of crops. The reason why they had done that is because they could hide in the tall crop; they can't be seen but they don't actually touch the ground. There are craft that do, but not theirs. He said they had been protecting this planet for thousands and thousands of years. He called the others 'devils' - the other two forms. He told me it was like a continual war with them. They are out to create trouble.

Mike: *For what purpose; did he say?*

He said, "They are just devils, manipulators. The word 'devil' derives from your Bible. You must remember that these people were only writing and describing what they saw; what their mind could take in. Your Bible describes angels, archangels and devils; a very good description of

18

beings which are in existence and have been for many thousands of years, described by people who did not understand what they saw. Our servants that we use for service, they are described as devils by many people. He told me that they, the Controllers, also had creatures to serve them but theirs would literally tear you apart if they could.

Mike: *Did he say what they looked like?*

Yes. They are like bears but not so large, never larger than about 4' 6". They wear no clothes. He told me that one had 'broken traces', as he put it, in Yorkshire; had escaped.

Did he say when?

That was 1964 and it was only a couple of years previously and they were still looking for it; he said it was in the Yorkshire Dales. They knew all our geography; they knew everything. There was nothing you could tell them, they knew everything. He asked me if I knew an area called Todmorden[4] and said it was there that one of the creatures had escaped. Some years ago, in the Yorkshire Post I think it was, there was a picture of a creature someone had photographed in the Yorkshire Dales, that matched the description he gave me, size, colouring, etc. A few weeks after, the body of a missing policeman was found on top of a slag heap which no one could have climbed; it must have been dropped. I went through to Todmorden to find out. It was hushed up. It had caused quite a stir. They had to get a helicopter to lift the body up. They held the funeral the same day. After the third meeting I went up to Todmorden several times and found that a strange creature had been seen, they even have photographs of it. I asked somebody for a description and it matched, the description matched. I tried to trace the policeman, but the police just laughed at me, although they did say strange things had happened there.

Going back to Frome where the main things happened; I went home that night from the hospital and thought about it. I thought about it for days. I kept saying to myself: "I am going! I'm not going! I am going!" but I don't know, something compelled me. So, I went.

[1] In his book *The Keepers*, Jim Sparks tells of how his experiences with off-worlders caused him to leave his home and keep moving from place to place, in the vain hope that they would not find him again.

[2] It does seem that 1999 saw an increase in natural disasters, compared to previous years and many of them have been recorded with terminology such as:
- 'one of the farthest north "progressive" derechos to have ever been recorded'
- 'It was among the largest Atlantic hurricanes of its strength ever recorded'
- 'Hurricane Floyd triggered the third largest evacuation in US history'
- The 1921 earthquake was the second-deadliest quake in recorded history in Taiwan
- Tropical Depression Eleven was a slow-moving system which caused some of the worst flooding in Mexico in over 50 years
- The 1999 Chamoli earthquake was the strongest to hit the foothills of the Himalayas in more than ninety years.
- The 1999 Hector Mine earthquake was a magnitude 7.1 earthquake that occurred on October 16, 1999 in a remote part of the Mojave Desert. The recurrence interval of large earthquakes in the Eastern California Shear Zone is considered to be in the order of thousands of years.

[3] It is not clear if George had taken his car to his daughter's home and left it there whilst he walked to the woods or had driven to the edge of the woods and parked or had, indeed, walked from Nunney to Frome and then to Longleat and, caught up in the tale, I forgot to ask. I have since lost touch with him. He said he was planning to walk home from Longleat. The distances are not too great by my estimation from just looking at a map (Nunney to Frome: approx. 3 miles; Frome to the forest approx. 3 miles and then approx. 4 miles back to Nunney) and for a local there may well have been shortcuts along lanes and across fields.

[4] Todmorden has been noted as an area of UFO activity and unusual sightings since the mid-1970s at least. See: http://www.disclose.tv/forum/the-bizarre-ufo-mystery-and-a-man-found-dead-england-t51348.html
http://www.ourufosociety.com/page/8/

Chapter 2
Assignation

I drove my car to the pub on the right-hand side of the road. I pulled in there. I don't drink. I went into the pub and asked for a double whiskey. I drank it neat. I didn't realise you put water with it. I came out. I drove up past the quarry gates before I realised I was there, so I decided to find a lay by. I couldn't find one, so I pulled in off the road, as far over as possible and I walked back. I glanced at my watch and it was a quarter to eight. The quarry gates were open but I decided not to go in. I think I was scared; it was lonely looking in there.

I walked slowly back towards the car. I lit a cigarette and leaned against a fence. Suddenly I heard a voice say, "Good evening! You're punctual!" I turned round and there he was.

I asked, "Where did you come from?"

He said, "Would you like to come with me?"

I said, "Yes, certainly."

We needed to be on the other side of the fence; I climbed over it but he actually jumped over it from a standing position. It was about three or four feet high. I said, "I wish I could do that!"

He said, "Oh anybody can do it if they want to! Come here, I have a surprise for you!"

Then I saw it in all its splendour - and it was big! I stopped still, because it was so incredible; it really was incredible.

Mike: *How big do you think it was?*

21

About forty feet. I said, "It's huge!"

He said, "This is only a small one. We have one not too far away which is probably, in your terms, three miles long."

I said, "Well, why can't people see it?"

"Sometimes it is much too far away, other times we create our own clouds, so if you sometimes see a dark cloud which seems to be going in the opposite direction to the rest, it will be one of our parent ships."

"What do you mean?"

"A parent ship carries two hundred of these craft."

"You mean there are over two hundred of these things flying around?"

"No, never more than twenty at a time and never more than three in one area."

"Have you ever had any accidents?"

"There have been accidents." He said they usually head for water. Incidentally, they have bases underwater; he told me that.

Mike: *Did he say where?*

Off the Welsh coast. There is a large island there, a large rock, which they actually fly straight into. Stack Rocks[5], that's it.

I asked him what he meant that they flew straight into it as it was solid rock. He said, "Is it solid? What is solid? How many dimensions do you have?"

"Three. I'm quite sure you know that."
"Three? Have you never asked yourself why there are not more?"

"I don't know."

"Because that is the extent of your knowledge. You have one dimension, you have two dimensions, you have three dimensions. Why shouldn't you have four dimensions, five dimensions, six dimensions?"

I said, "Well, I can't see that!"

"Fortunately, you can't, but there are. You could move into another dimension quite simply. We do it often."

"Does that explain your invisible craft on your previous visit?"

"Exactly."

"So, I was in another dimension?"

"You were. It didn't affect you, did it?"

"No."

"It's quite simple really. When we want to disappear, we just move into another dimension. All the people who talk about us, who try to track us, especially your very, very childish radar - we can move off their screens anytime we wish just by going into another dimension; they can't follow us. When you read reports of us just disappearing off the radar screen, it is simply because we have gone into another dimension - and you could do it as well.

I said, "Why don't you show me how?"

"Because it is much too complicated for you now, but it can be done and we do it regularly. Now, you asked me last time, because you were interested, how long it took us to travel from our galaxy to yours?"

"Yes."

"No time at all, because we are in the same galaxy. The earth is part of the Milky Way galaxy; it's the same galaxy."

"How long does it take you to travel?"

"We never do it straight, we have bases. We do a hop and a hop and a hop." He knew all the characteristics of the English language. He was able to sometimes even use slang. He said that the moon base was the easiest because it took them two hours of earth time to come to the earth's atmosphere.[6]

I asked, "Is that another dimension?"

"No. There's a limit to speed; once you go over that limit you are virtually in a time-warp. You have a saying on your planet that we laugh at on many occasions: that somebody is in such a hurry that they meet themselves coming back. Speed is completely and totally irrelevant. If you left one of your airports to fly to Amsterdam it would take you approximately 45 minutes, correct?"

I said, "Yes. I've flown from London to Amsterdam."

"So, if you leave at four your time you land in Amsterdam at a quarter to five, correct?"

"No. You arrive at a quarter to six because they are an hour ahead of us."

He said, "Thank you. Now think backwards. Leave Amsterdam at five, it's three quarters of an hour to London, what time do you arrive?"
"A quarter of an hour before I left!"

"Think about it. Time is irrelevant. Speed is irrelevant. Our craft are capable of..."

"Of what?"

"Aah! That will come at a later date." But he never did tell me.

He continued, "Let's put it this way: I could take off in this craft now and before you could snap your fingers I've gone; I've disappeared."

I said, "Is that speed?"

He said, "You call it speed. That's not what we call it. We call it propulsion."

I said, "But two hours from the moon?"

"Yes."
"Doesn't it affect your body or anything?"

"No!"

"I just don't get it. Is the inside of your body the same as ours?"

"Oh yes! Exactly the same. Even our brain is the same as yours; the only difference is that whereas we use most of our brain's functions,
you only use a very small part. You should look at your brain as a computer. To build a computer with the same capacity as your brain you would need to have a building

the size of a very large city. That is its capacity - and you don't use it because you have forgotten how. There was a time when it was used."

Mike: *Did he say when that was?*

Yes. He didn't say the exact time. He said, "One of the things which intrigues our learned people is the belief that the people on your planet have that you have only existed for a few thousand years. My friend, you have existed for trillions of years, trillions. We have had many discussions with our learned ones about theories that have been put forward on your world, such as that you evolved from fish. This is utterly nonsensical because human beings came before anything else. Animals, as you call them, came later. Humans were the first inhabitants. You destroyed your planet on numerous occasions. By that, I mean you destroyed the living conditions on your planet and it took many, many years to recover from that. I will give you a 'for instance': When your scientists were going to explode their first atomic weapon, they were looking for an area which was safe. They searched high and low and found a desert, which you call the Mohave Desert. The scientists discovered, when they dug down and down, they came to molten green glass. They used carbon dating to date this. It was ten million years old! They should have been warned! When they dropped their first atomic bomb, they dropped it from above the ground and the area below it turned into green, molten glass. Do you understand what I am trying to tell you?"

"That it has happened before?"

"Yes!"

He said we had destroyed the planet time and time again. During our talks he brought up the Bible time and again. He said, "If you were to take your Bible and read it in just plain, everyday language, you would be surprised what you would uncover. You'll uncover spaceships - ours. In one part of your Bible, you have a story about Ezekiel's wheel of fire. We have spaceships like that. You read about Moses and the Mount; Moses coming down with his instructions. Wasn't that a spaceship?"

I said, "I don't know."

He said, "It was. You have a man who has been traced down the centuries, who always turns up; who always has the same name, and shortly afterwards science makes tremendous advances because this person gives them his knowledge. You know who I am talking about. He is one of us. His main job is to come here when he is needed."

He went on, "In the past two years you have made tremendous scientific strides. Does nobody have the sense to stand still and ask: 'Why so suddenly?' Because we have given you the means to help yourselves to try and deter these other beings, plus we are also trying to help you stave off what looks inevitable - the destruction of your planet. Not that it would be entirely destroyed; there would still be life, but not much, and it will build up again as it has done before. It happens regularly."

I said, "You talk like this but how old are you?"

"I wondered how long it would take you to ask that question! Your year is 354 days; ours is 257 days. I'll explain that sometime - but therefore our year is less than yours, but our life span is 500 years."

"You live to 500?"

"Yes, many of our people do. But that is only about 350 of your years."

"How do you manage to live that long?"

"Because we have perfected the means of renewing organs in our bodies. We have also given your people that opportunity. You have expanded your life spans, yet you keep destroying yourselves. You have more poisons in your atmosphere, which is why we can remain no longer than 24 hours. But the poisons in your atmosphere are destroying the life on your world.

You see these trees and bushes? Tomorrow, come here; walk, look at the trees, look at the bark on the trees, look at the leaves on the trees. Do the same with the bushes. If you have the time, count how many leaves there are on a bush, count how many dead and dying leaves there are. It is your atmosphere, poisoning every living thing.

Now you look on life as just being human life. This is wrong. Animal life is life; vegetation is life. You are destroying the very thing which is meant to make you live. You are spending a lot of time destroying it. We have got people on your world at the moment, many hundreds of people, trying to get that message across but nobody will listen because a few of your top people are under the control of these other beings from our galaxy. They are intent on only power, wealth and greed. Nothing else matters to them and they are fully aware that they are actually destroying themselves and their descendants. We cannot understand that way of thinking. If people were to listen, just listen, and try to do something, who knows? A few years ago, if you lived to be sixty of your years, you would be very lucky. Now you have people living to be ninety or a hundred years old. Why do you not stop and think? You have improved your life span but you are still going to destroy it because of your stupidity.

The last time we met I showed you some pictures. They were taken inside your world. Your world is porous, very much so. Common sense will tell you that your planet is made up of various minerals, etc. Why are you destroying it? You cannot keep taking away something which has taken millions of years to get there and expect it to replenish itself in a day or two. It just does not happen. You keep destroying yourselves and you are alarming us. What you have done now is worse than anything you have ever done before and that is that you have a safety layer above your planet which also protects the other parts of your galaxy, including us. You call it the Van Allen Belt. You are destroying it at an alarming rate. So now your poisons are escaping into the stratosphere; eventually they will find their way to our world and to other worlds."

I said, "Are there other worlds?"

"Many. Why should you think that you are the only beings? If I told you how many planets there are: there are millions of planets capable of sustaining life in this galaxy and there are many other galaxies."

"If everything is so good on your world, why do you come here?"
"Because if you destroy your world, you destroy ours. It is as simple as that. We do not like wars; we have beaten wars. We now have a war against two other intelligent life forms, but not a war as you know it. We do not shoot each other or kill each other; we try to prevent each other. We are trying to prevent them. They are not using guns or technological weapons, they are using more insidious ways of creating wars, by getting the people to fight amongst themselves and destroy themselves."

That's what he said is happening to us. He added:

"There is only one thing I will warn you about and that is that I know you will not tell anyone about this."

"Are you warning me now?"

"No, you are free to say what you wish, to whom you wish but we hope it will be directed to the proper channels. However, that is quite difficult, so we know that you will not go talking to just anyone about it."

"Is there anyone who would stop me?"

"There might be. There might be."

"Explain that please."

"Well, all human beings, including ourselves, are a source of electrical power, so therefore, if we want to find you again at a later date, we can find you."

"How?"

"Call it a form of radar. We know your frequency now. It will be quite simple to tune into it because you are all different; that's what human beings are, everyone is different, but you are a source of electrical power; you have electrical impulses coming from you every second, so therefore we can trace you."

This is one of the reasons why I disappeared.

The being said, "You might talk at length about it but don't be surprised if it appears as though you have a memory lapse or a block."

"Why, is it something you have done?"

"No, we have not harmed you. We have no intentions of harming you, as you are fully aware."

"These electrical impulses, can you control them?

"If we wish. Everything is stored in your brain; everything, until the day you die. It is all stored there, but it can be wiped."

When I've thought back over what he said I've explained it to myself this way: the brain is a computer; a computer is a memory bank, so is the brain. You can either have total recall or your computer could become faulty. Sometimes it becomes faulty because of a bug, a computer bug. I think he was implying that they can put the equivalent of a bug into our brain to stop us recalling things. I said to him, 'But I don't want to forget this'."

"You will never forget this but sometimes, if you talk about it, you must make sure that you are in the right, receptive company. That is vitally important to you because one sceptic amongst those people can cause your memory to be erased forever."

"That doesn't sound possible."

"Does it sound possible to come from the moon to the earth in two hours?"

"I get the point."

"You think too many things are impossible. I'll give you a little saying for you to remember: 'some things are highly improbable but nothing is impossible'."

That night I got two glasses of the green liquid. I enjoyed it. It tasted like a fruit jelly only half set.

Mike: *Any taste that you recognised?*

No. Just very nice. Very refreshing. That lifted me up; all tiredness left me. Then he told me that it was time they were going. We went outside and I reminded him that he was going to show me something.

"Come with me." We walked right up to the tip of the quarry.

"Please, we'll meet again two nights from tonight, same time, same place. I know you'll be there."

"I will."

"Now please go down and just wait there."

So, I went down. All of a sudden, this huge thing just came over and came right down until it was about twenty or thirty feet above me. There were three huge, circular, what looked like, balls. There were no windows, by the way. I didn't see any windows on any of the three occasions. It just suddenly went to the side. He explained why they went to the side on the third visit. He also explained why there were no windows when it was in flight.

They went to the side quite a distance, then shot straight up, without a sound of any kind. He told me that if they had gone up when they were above me, they would have fragmented me, blown me to smithereens, so they moved to the side. The velocity they needed to take off was so great that anything below it would have got the full blast. They go to the side first to find a clear space with a solid surface as that helps them to lift off.

Mike: *Did he ever mention anything about the craft creating a vacuum in front of it?*

Yes. On the third visit, but I'll tell you briefly. The craft actually drags itself forward. It fits into itself, but it is done with such a rapid movement that it looks like one movement. He explained that method of propulsion to me.

That is why they can reach the speeds they do, because there is a vacuum and they create the vacuum in front of them."

Mike: *Did he mention anything about cathode rays?*

No. Never. He did say that they can take television pictures anywhere in the world, even pinpointed to one room in a house. He said they could do this either from their craft or from their own planet?

Here I should explain that George came to us in a state of some distress, wanting to finally tell someone the whole story he carried within him. He had been 'on the run' for some years (more about that later) and as he talked and began to relax into his story, we all felt that what he had said so far was only the tip of the tale. Even more amazing revelations were waiting in the wings - and then they came...

---

[5] Stack Rocks and the craft that fly in and out of them are mentioned in the books *The Welsh Triangle* by Peter Paget and *The Dyfed Enigma* by Randall Pugh. In 1977 the area, and Ripperston Farm in particular, became the centre of both a UFO 'flap' and a series of strange occurrences.

[6] In his book *Millennial Hospitality*, written in 2002, Charles Hall tells how the 'Tall White' aliens took the US Generals for short trips to the moon and back.

Chapter 3
Men in Black and a Meal on a Spaceship

After a break for coffee and cookies, George continued his tale:

From what I was told, especially on the third visit, I am terrified of what is going to happen, because what he told me then, in 1964, has come true with such incredible accuracy that I can't believe it. There is a lot more to come and it is coming so fast it is quite incredible.

He told me about these people; he said, "You call them prophets but why should one person have knowledge of the future unless they know something that you don't? All events that happen are planned, organised, engineered and executed at the right time. Everything is going to a plan, a Master Plan. Your life is one big Master Plan, ours is the same, but whereas we have learned to control what happens, you haven't because you have too many divisions in your world. Whereas our world is controlled by just a few, your world is controlled by so many who do not trust each other, who do not believe each other and whose priorities are power and wealth. We do not have this on our world. Money is a word your world invented. Have you ever thought about what happened before money was invented? You bartered. We still barter. We do not have money. We do not have banks as you have banks. We have no trouble because we do not deal in money."

George paused and took a gulp from a glass of water beside him.

Mike: *Go on*

I didn't keep the fourth appointment, which was to be in February. I thought about it. I started having nightmares.

Two people came to the door one day and asked for me by name. I was out at the time. They came back that night. I saw them come up the garden path. They looked like two Mormons to me. They looked at me and said, "I hope you remember that you mustn't talk about what you have seen and heard. Alright?" And they walked off.

We had a big house and it was on a corner. To reach it you would have to park your car in a lay-by and walk up the lane, then turn right to the big path, so it would take a bit of time for you to walk it. I ran down and saw nothing, not even a car. The road is straight down - but there was nothing.

Houses in Nunney

Then on the Sunday afternoon these two men walked up to me as I was about to get into my car and said, "Good afternoon. I hope you have remembered what you were told."

I said, "Who the hell are you?"
One said, "That doesn't really matter. Just remember, keep what you have seen and been told all to yourself and nothing will happen to your family."

That happened six or seven times altogether. For the sake of my family, I packed up and went. I moved to Manchester. I got a house there. I left my wife our house. I gave her my bank book. I gave her everything and I went off. I ran for my life, knowing full well I couldn't run away really. I left my children - and they're all very close to me. I have six lovely daughters, three sons, seventeen grandchildren and four great grandchildren and it worries me when I know they are not going to have a very good life ahead of them.

Mike: *Can we change things?*

Yes. We can change it. This is why I am trying to get all this off my chest. I wrote to the Ministry of Defence. I have a good war record and I thought they would pay attention to me. I wrote to the Prime Minister, Mrs Thatcher. I wrote to the Air Ministry. I wrote to an organisation called Justice. Not even an acknowledgement."

How much did you tell them?

I gave a very brief resume, about two pages of foolscap, in which I gave them approximate dates, months and years of things I knew were going to happen and what is still to happen. They, the space people, told me in 1964 that the 70s, 80s and 90s would be the years of poison. They told me that a source of energy would be cut off in one fell swoop, any time from 1999 onwards; but I'll go back and try and tell you things in order.

About halfway through the second visit he apologised to me and asked if I wanted anything to eat. They brought out some plates, which appeared to be ordinary plastic, a big bowl, and then ladled out what appeared to be white meat. I don't know what it was. All they gave me was what looked like a short knitting needle with a pointed end. I watched the woman and she dug it in the food and just picked it up and put it in her mouth. I did the same. We had the same green drink. It wasn't sickly, it wasn't sweet; it was very refreshing and seemed to give a lift. We spent about fifteen to twenty minutes eating, without a word being said. I couldn't finish it. It was very filling or I wasn't as hungry as I thought I was. There was no bread or vegetables or condiments or anything like that, just the bare food on the plate.

The woman took it away and we continued the conversation we had been having about the interior of the world, and he started talking about the outside of the planet and how we are destroying both. He explained to me that the damage was being done because of greed in destroying 'living creatures' which breathe in the poisons and exude pure oxygen. He asked why people were doing this when they know what they are doing. Then the woman came back in again. All the time we were talking, the three creatures were standing against the wall; they never said anything. Then, abruptly, he cut everything short and said, "We must go now, but we can arrange to meet again. Same place, same time." And that was the end of the second visit.

On the Thursday night, the ten o'clock News was on the radio that was still on and I had gone out just before eight. My watch had stopped at half-past eight. Then I went to bed and, without a word of a lie, I went out like a light. When I woke the next morning I thought, *"God, what a dream that was!"* I got up, my wife was downstairs, my kids had gone to school so I went to the bathroom to wash. When I undressed there were blisters everywhere; everywhere covered! Anyway, when I put my clothes on it didn't show so I thought I would give it a day and if it got no better, I would have to go and see a doctor. But the following day they had faded to just brown marks; they had not burst. I still have many of the brown marks. I remember that well; it was a Thursday and the final meeting was on the Saturday of the week after.

The next time, I walked to the quarry, as it was not far from the car park. Again, I stood at the same place; there was nothing in sight. It was a very dark night; raining, drizzling. The agreed time of 8 p.m. came and went. I was just about to give up when, again, a voice spoke to me: "Stay!"

I turned round. There was no one. I thought I was hearing things. A lot of queer things had been happening which made me question my own mind, my sanity. I was just about to walk away when a hand touched my shoulder and he said, "We have had a slight delay. Come this way." Again, he jumped the fence. He just seemed to hop over it while I had to climb.

We walked right round the quarry and up; this time he was leading me. This time I watched him; he did not take steps as we do; he seemed to be gliding. I was fascinated. His legs were not moving at all. He was slightly off the ground. I don't know, he must have been, it was rough terrain. I went up and by the time we had got up the hill I was a bit breathless. He turned and apologised immediately, saying: "Oh, I'm sorry! Rest!"

So, I rested and all the while I looked down to see if I could see the craft. I didn't see anything. We kept on walking. He told me to wait - and then it just glided over, not a sound; a gorgeous sight.

Mike: *The same one as before?*

Well, it looked the same. It was the same size. It just came down. The door opened; it opened down. Inside was a light, a diffused light. It was a very strong light but it didn't hurt the eyes. He took my arm and we went in. He must have lifted me about three feet (1 metre) to get in because the craft was hovering about that height from the ground.

Inside was a bare room but this time he took me right to the top of the craft. There were another two men. At the top it was all windows, which I didn't see before from the outside; all little round windows. He said, "This is our Control."

I asked if they understood me and he replied, "No, only I understand you."
"Why are you showing me this?"

"Because you showed curiosity on your last visit. I don't suppose you understand anything here?"

I said, "No."

There seemed to be only a few instruments. He saw the look on my face and said, "It is different to what you expected?"

"I thought it would be a mass of high-tech equipment."

"Why?"

"Because this is a high-tech thing, isn't it?"

He could not understand this and was really puzzled. I said, "Well, the distance you travel and the conditions you travel under."

"There is no reason why it should not be simplified. No, we do not need many instruments; we don't need much high-tech equipment. I can't tell you all about our energy source, but it is supplied; we pick it up as we go along."

"You told me about lines that you travel on."

"Yes, that is correct. We travel on certain lines. Can I ask you a question? How many times have you heard of our craft being seen?"

"Lots of times. I've read it in the papers, (During this period local papers were running accounts of UFO sightings) but a lot of it I don't believe."

"Why not? You believe in our craft?"

"I've got to now; I'm in one!"

"How do you know you are in one?"

"We are talking in riddles here now."

When I said 'riddles' it was one word which seemed to have him beat. He said, "Just a moment. What do you mean by riddles?" I had to explain.

Then he said, "There is no purpose to be achieved up here. You wanted to see it the last time and I am letting you see it. We cannot disturb the crew; they are working at the moment. Contrary to what you might think, all the time we are here they have to keep their eyes on the controls."

So, then we came down to the second level. The inside of the craft seemed much larger than it looked from the outside. He said, "Would you like to listen for a moment?" A couple of minutes went by then he looked at me and said, "Well?"

"What am I listening for?"

"Can't you hear anything at all?"

"No."

"Would it surprise you to know that your domestic animals and your beasts of the field can hear something? Our motors are functioning but human ears do not seem to be able to pick it up, but your animals do."

"Oh."

"It was an experiment. Our motors are on at the moment."

"Now you told me that your propulsion was a natural propulsion, so where do motors come in?"

"I am using a term that you use on your planet. You would call it an engine but we don't use engines as you would imagine them. Our 'engine' is natural power, natural resources. We harness nature."

"Why can't we do that?"
"You are doing it, but you are doing it wrongly. I asked you a question, which you didn't answer properly. Where would you say the greatest number of sightings of our craft are?"

"Somerset is one, Wiltshire another. I can't think of any other."

"If I say over your electricity power stations; would you say they have been seen there regularly?"

"I don't know. Why do you ask me that question?"

"I just wanted to see if you knew anything about that."

"No. Are you trying to tell me that you...."?

"I didn't say anything. Let's change the subject. You don't know; therefore, it would be better if you did not know. We are going to sit down. We must have a long talk, because this is the last time I can see you for at least 56 to 60 days."

"Why?"

"We must go back to my world. We have been here too long. So, we are leaving during your night to go back."

"How long will that take you?"

"Three of your days."

"In this?"

"No. We re-join our parent ship."

"The one you described? It is just for one craft?"

"I didn't say that. There are many of our craft."

"Is there a possibility I can see this parent craft?"

"Sometime in the future, probably. I will promise you. Not now. Preparations have gone ahead for us to go back to our planet and we must have, as I said, 56 or 60 days there before we can come back."

"We haven't talked very much this time about anything."

"What do you want to know? Ask me."

"No. You were going to tell me things. I can't ask you anything because I don't know what to ask."

"Would you like to know what is going to happen on your world?"

"What do you mean 'what is going to happen'?"

"Oh, we can tell you what is going to happen and we can tell you approximately when."

"Well, I am interested."

And that is the point where he came to tell me about the end of this century and after 2,000; that is when our planet ends.

I said, "Is it going to be destroyed by war or something?"

"No. It is from outer space, away from our galaxy completely. It is already on the way. It happened before and it is going to happen again."

"I don't understand that."

"It will be a natural disaster. In your year 1999, in the middle of that year, there will be a solar event that will herald a chain of catastrophes that will have far-reaching consequences[7]. These will not be natural catastrophes; your people created the causes themselves. They are in the process of doing it now and unless someone reverses what has started, there is no stopping it."

"I thought you people were able to stop things?"

"No. We will not interfere. We have never interfered. It is wrong to interfere. The only thing we can do is to stop those that try to control from doing too much damage, but we can't prevent everything. They have already taken control of your world in the high places. If they are not in the high places, they are dominating people in high places; these people are making decisions not realising

43

the consequences. We cannot interfere with that. We cannot interfere with anything that is going to happen; the only people who can are your people. We have talked to many of your people; many hundreds of your people, but your authorities refuse to act."

He told me that on one occasion his people met with officials from a certain nation; he did not say which nation. They were taken prisoner and the craft was taken as well, but they died. He said, "Because we cannot live in your atmosphere for too long; it is poisonous." I asked him what sort of atmosphere he had on his planet.

"An oxygen mix, the same as you. If you were living on your planet 1500 years ago you would have been breathing very good oxygen; today you are not. You are breathing a percentage of oxygen and a high percentage of poison. You do not realise that you are killing yourselves."

At this point the girl came in and I asked what age she was. I thought she was about twenty. She was seventy years old. She had long, fair hair and a very slim figure. I never once saw them without this dull, metallic, one-piece outfit. Only twice did I see them with the hoods on. I didn't see zips or clips of any kind. This was a tight hood, it just showed the face and only on three occasions did I see any of them with the hood off, just lying loose at the back.

The girl came in and it was explained to me they would like me to make love to her. He said, "The reason is your seed. We have done this before; we have many thousands of children born of human parents and a lot of them are back on your world now, doing good. We can move into your world by simple bodily restructuring but because of your atmosphere we have to wear artificial means of protection which would be very obvious."

That's when they showed me the belt they wear. He said, "We have to wear this at all times. In simple terms it is our life-support system"

He took me to the second floor again. The woman and one of the other men were releasing what looked like soap bubbles from a machine. He saw the look on my face and said, "Ask the question that you want to ask."

"What are these?"

"They send back pictures."

"To the craft?"

"No. To our world. Everything is recorded. Each one picks up sound and pictures and they can go where we cannot go. That is why I am able to speak your language and why I understand what is happening. We know it all. Now these will scatter all over the country. When they are finished with, we burst them. It's quite simple: once we switch off the system, they burst, like your soap bubbles, and there is no trace. That is how we get our information. We cannot land in the high street on your towns. You may wonder why we don't. I'll ask you a question. Suppose three of our craft came to one of your major towns or cities and we decided to land. What would happen?"

"I don't really know."

"I can tell you what would happen: with the mentality that your people have, you would panic; there would be shooting, there would be destruction, because the first thing they will think of is: 'That's not right. Destroy it before it destroys us!' Even though we come in peace. That's the reason, the only reason, why we do not do such a thing. But one day, one day, we will come in force."
"To invade?"

"No. To aid. I told you, from the year 1999 onwards your planet will get into deeper trouble." He brought up the matter again of the year's length and the age in which we live. "There was a period on your planet when you did live to be 500 years old, 700 of our years."

"What happened?"

"A very good question. You destroyed yourselves. We have watched you with interest over the centuries. You made an effort but the effort ceased. Just a few years ago for some reason, you came to a dead end, you decided it wasn't worth the trouble, so you are now reverting and you are now going to bring on centuries-old diseases that you had once conquered, they are going to return."

He did not use the word 'Aids' but described a disease that sounded like it. The last time it had been heard of was when Cain and Abel were alive, because Abel had been a sufferer. I said that he was now going back a long time and he said, "You have read about it in your holy book. You have read about Lot's wife, haven't you? Your ancient people were not very good at describing things and said she was turned into a pillar of salt. My friend, many, many years ago you carried out atomic experiments on your world and the people who took part in those experiments were told to turn their backs to it. The atomic bombs that you dropped on your world recently surprised us very much. We thought you would know of the devastating effect they can have on your environment. Your world is just as though it were encased in a bubble; everything that is released in your atmosphere cannot escape so it is going around and around. The residue is left to poison your world. Even our craft, to leave your world have to reach a certain velocity and for ten to fifteen minutes of your time we are in a red-hot craft. Nothing else can escape. It is artificial velocity which allows us to escape. So, what do you think happens to all the poisonous gases, etc., that you allow into the atmosphere? Where do you think they are going? They cannot go anywhere. They are enclosed in a bubble, captive and must eventually sink."

He asked me about my family, if I had discussed this with them. I said I had not and he asked me why not. "Because you asked me not to and I think I would be laughed out of existence."

"Human frailty. You are afraid of being thought different."

"I am afraid of being thought a head case." I had to explain that to him.

"Yes. I can believe that. We have studied a lot of your books which have been published about our so-called presence. They describe us, but they don't describe the Controllers. Why?"

"Because people think there is only you lot - and even then, I'm not too sure."

"Are you convinced that we are from another place?"

"I'm convinced that you are from another place, but you are so normal."

"Thank you."

"I'm serious. We are talking now as I talk to friends."

"We are friends."

"Yes, I'm quite sure of that. However, if I were to repeat this to anyone, they would say that there is something wrong with me; they would say I was mentally deranged, that there is something wrong with my head."

"Yes, I can understand that. That is human frailty. People are not prepared to believe something that is beyond their understanding, their limited understanding. Which is why, if anything happens, we get the blame. My friend, I can assure you that we have done more to assist progress on your world by now and again giving a prod to your scientists to point them in the right direction, seeing that they get certain information to help them. Stop and think how fast, with what speed, technology and medicine have come to your world. There have been rapid strides in the last ten years of your time. For centuries we have turned up on the scene when your people had an idea and we would point them in the right direction. Sometimes the knowledge was used for the wrong purpose, which we regret very, very much."

"I thought you said you didn't interfere."

"We don't make things happen. We don't force action, but we do make some information that your scientists are discovering clearer, in the hope that they will choose rightly. Your people are always left with free choice."

George then remarked to Mike that he had still not sorted out in his mind the nature of 'interference' and a lively discussion followed as to what does, and what does not, constitute interference between one species and another. You, no doubt, have your own opinions. In the end, if we each look within, we know that, whatever our circumstances, we have choices. Read on and you will see how vital it is that we each exercise that ability wisely. Indeed, it is our serious responsibility so to do.

[7]A total solar eclipse occurred on August 11, 1999 with an eclipse magnitude of 1.029. It was the first total eclipse visible from Europe since July 22, 1990, and the first visible in the United Kingdom since June 29, 1927. Wikipedia says: "Because of the high density populated in the areas of the path, there is little doubt that this was the most-viewed total solar eclipse in human history."

Chapter 4
Predictions, Prophecies and Plain Talking

The taping of George's tale took place once a week over a period of six weeks or so. He had much to tell and most of it had been bottled up for years. Often, as his story unfolded, he would be overcome by emotion and we would need to stop the interview for a while or altogether for that session. Sometimes memories would surface that he had not recalled at all over the years until that moment. Much of what he had to say sounded bizarre, as many UFO experiences do if judged within the parameters of accepted 'normality'. Many points correlated with data collected from other sources over the years; some things he claimed to have been told could now be disproved with the passing of time; some had proven to be true, others pointed to the future - and it to those we now come.

A new tape was put into the machine and George continued his story.

He showed me, on a screen, pictures of different types of craft, all from this galaxy, the Milky Way.

Mike: *Did he give a name to his planet?*

It was 'X' something, that's all I remember. He did tell me but I can't remember it. He said it can be seen from Earth. He told me it took them three days and nights to get here in their parent craft.

Mike: *Did he say how fast they went?*

He had no idea of speed, that was the peculiar thing. He never spoke of miles per hour or minutes, etc. He said, "Speed is something that we don't even think about. Our parent ship at the moment is about three thousand miles out in space, waiting. When we give the signal it will come down, to just above the Van Allen Belt. We fly straight into our parent craft."

He showed me moving pictures of the inside of this massive craft. There was row upon row of these objects and two went in while we were watching. They looked minute going in and there were rows and rows of them. He told me there were many thousands of their craft. He said, "We have a mother craft above your Pacific Ocean; we have another above your Atlantic Ocean. When we get the signal the parent craft may be two thousand miles away. It will take about five minutes to reach it. We have some way to go in this conversation as it is the last, as I told you before, for 56 to 60 days. We won't be leaving until about one o'clock your time."

"You know the time?"

"Of course, we know the time."

"Do you have time on your planet?"

"Yes, we do, but not in the same context. It is too complicated to go into at this point but one day we will discuss that and I'll explain our measurement of time elapsing and how it differs from yours, very slightly. We would rather work on your understanding now so that you can understand what I am trying to say to you. My superiors have agreed with me that, if you agree, we will take you and let you see your world from a height of two thousand miles."

"What do you mean by that?"

"If you agree, only if you agree, we will take you above your world and bring you back to this spot."

"How long will that take?"

"I think I just explained to you."

"Won't I have to wear something?"

"No. This is all self-contained. You are completely protected. If you don't want to, please say so, but I know you have a very inquisitive mind and I think you want to."

"I'm not too sure."

"We have some time. Think about it; we'll come back to it. Is there something you wanted to know especially?"

"Yes. When is our planet going to end? In1999?"

"No. There will be major catastrophes all over.....Just a moment."

He went out and came back with the girl who was carrying a flat-looking thing. She sat down. He spoke to her in the clicking noise. Then he turned to me: "Now, repeat what you want to know."

"Is our planet going to end in 1999?"

"No. It will be at the beginning of the second century, after the year 2000."

"Do you mean in 2000?"

"In between 2100 and 2150. 95% of your life will be extinct. Human and otherwise."

"Because of the poison in the atmosphere?"

"No. From a source outside your system completely, which is now on its way. It has been on its way for many thousands of years but we have calculated when it will reach your earth."
"This sounds fantastic!"

"It is fantastic my friend! When you think that when that object hits your world it will have trillions of the power of the nuclear bombs you are trying to perfect now!"
"So, it is destined to end?"

"No. Your world will go on but only 5% of life, all life, will survive. It happened before; it will happen again. It is a cycle which cannot be stopped."

"Is it an artificial object?"

"No. It is a collision which is happening every minute in outer space. There are trillions and trillions and trillions of planets, stars and asteroids flying around the atmosphere outside our galaxy. There must be collisions. The world will never end but 95% of life will be finished. It has happened before and those who were left took thousands of years to develop and regain some of the knowledge they had before. Even you have not regained full knowledge. You have not regained the full use of your brain and you will not live long enough to regain that power; you won't be allowed to. That is the nature of things.

Your year now is 1964 on your world. From the year 1970 you will begin to experience natural calamities, gigantic ones: tidal waves, earthquakes, volcanic eruptions. They will be increasing in intensity and in time they will happen regularly, more regularly than ever before, because of what you are doing to the interior of your own planet. You are creating that. There is no way it can be stopped now. Therefore, you will have famine, you will have drought, you will have every known catastrophe that nature can provide, but you have created it yourselves and there is nothing we can do to help, absolutely nothing."

"So, from 1970 we are going to be in for a rough ride?"
"Much rougher than you imagine. It will escalate into the 1990s and the next century and those years will become increasingly difficult for you. A lot of the troubles in that period will be engineered by the Controllers; will be controlled by people under their control on your own planet. People who will be obsessed, because the idea will be placed in their minds, by wealth and power; nothing else will matter. The needs of the few will surpass those of the many. Do you understand that?"

"Yes, very well. So, things are going to get worse?"

"Much worse. There will be starvation. Millions will die on a planet of plenty because the needs of the few are considered more highly than the needs of the many. You will be trusting people that you should not trust, because even they do not know they are being controlled by the manipulators."

"Why can't you stop these Controllers?"

"We do not believe in wars, as you do. We do not believe in violence or force. We try other means. They are successful to a certain degree, but only to a certain degree. In any case, our superiors will not let us interfere in the progress of the galaxy. The Controllers look after their part in the galaxy very successfully. We look after our part in the galaxy very successfully. You are the only ones not being successful because you are not even trying. You don't want to try. I am sorry I have to say this to you, but you have to try and get that message across. Unless people will sharpen their minds and memories and remember and keep remembering and stop the rot that has set in on your world...."

"Are we talking about this country, Great Britain?"

"No, I am talking about your world. Every country on your planet is exactly the same. They have been taken over by the few. I know that one person cannot do that much but we have told many people this, many high officials; we have many allies in high places but even they don't seem to have the power to stop the rot that is going on. It is going to escalate and escalate until the early part of the next century, when you will find that 45% of your world will cease to exist. What concerns us most is that you, yourselves are doing it. No outside source; you are doing it. The Controllers advise, they control minds, but you, the majority, are the people who can stop it but you won't even try."

Then he returned to the subject of me going for a trip with them. I said, "No!"

"You told me once that you had flown in your last war. Why are you afraid now?"

"Because this isn't like an aeroplane!"

"Why? In what way is it different?"

"The shape for one thing."

"You have some odd shaped aeroplanes. You have V-shaped aeroplanes. We have V-shaped craft. So, what is the difference?"

"I don't know. There don't seem to be many instruments up there. No controls either."

"Are we talking about accidents?"

"Yes. By the way, have you had any accidents?"

"Very, very few."

"I have heard of them coming down into the sea. Isn't that an accident?"

"No. We have undersea bases. Because it is sealed, the craft is shielded against the element of water as well."

"By the way, do you have water on your world?"

"Not as you know it. You've drunk our water with a chemical added, which we have to put in because we cannot drink it otherwise."

"That was water I was drinking?"

"Yes, water, but with a chemical added to make it drinkable. Otherwise, it would taste of sulphur. When you leave the craft later on, if you agree to come with us, you will smell that sulphur because sulphur is one of our main elements. Will you come with us?"

"Yes - but I will be coming back?"

"Oh yes. The only people who come with us are those who wish to come. It is just a short trip. While we are talking, you haven't asked me the obvious question as to where are our windowlets."

"Don't you have them?"

"Oh yes. You'll see them."

"When?"

"I think now is as good a time as any."

55

Chapter 5
Beyond Earth

He looked at the girl and said something; she went out. Then the whole side seemed to split open to show a row of perfectly round windows.

He said, "Come here a moment. Have a look at your world."

By that time, I think I was panic stricken. I said, "Have we been on the way all the time?"

"Only when you agreed to come. We are about two thousand miles above your world. Does it not look lovely?"

And it does.

It is very difficult to describe it. It is blue with a greenish tinge in areas; a bright blue, a beautiful blue. It is gorgeous-looking. You can see the clouds; you can see everything. It has a lump at the bottom towards the right. It is pear-shaped slightly to the side. I thought he was pulling my leg. It was barely five minutes since I had agreed. He said, "Don't you remember I told you how long it would take to reach the parent ship?"

"Where is the parent ship now?"

"It is on its way but it is too far away. I cannot take you any further, we have to go back now and I must close these. Do you want to have another look?"

I looked but I still could not believe it. I said, "How do I know that is real?"

"How do we know it is real! We have not done this for a while. Wait a moment; I'll prove it to you!"
He went out and came back within a few seconds and said, "Now, stand here with me."

So, I stood beside him. "Watch your planet!"

I watched. Suddenly it seemed to be darting about the sky, then it disappeared. I had to look through another window to see it again. I asked him what had happened.

"We did a bit of a run-around, a bit of manoeuvring. We placed the planet in another position for you. Now we will go down, pass your planet and come back in, but we must close first."

The windows were closed. I never felt any movement, nothing at all.

Within a couple of minutes he said, "Right!" He spoke to the girl again and the windows opened.

He said, "Look at that side. You have seen the same continents because we are keeping pace with your world, so you have seen the same situations. We are going to go round and you'll see your different continents. You will recognise your continents; you have seen them in your school atlases; you must have."

"You know about school atlases?"

"Of course, we do, and your maps, etc. You will know what your continents look like?"

"Of course, I do."

"So, what is the main continent you can see there at the moment?"

"It looks like Australia, New Zealand and Japan."

"Right. So now you will want to see your own section."

Again, there was the wavering sensation, then I could see Great Britain quite plainly, and France, right down to Italy, the leg, and North Africa as plain as anything. It was a bluish colour."

"Are you satisfied now, because we have to go?"

"Yes."

"Would you like a drink?"

"Oh, yes please."

So, he brought me again that same drink. It only takes a couple of minutes to have a drink. He said, "Right." Again, he clicked something to the girl. And the windows opened. I looked outside and there was total darkness. I asked where we were now.

"Back where we started."

"What, on the ground?"

"Not far off it; two or three feet."

"You said 'feet', don't you use metric measure?"

"If you wish. We are approximately one metre from your surface."

"I can't beat you, can I?"

"I would hardly think so. Anyway, are you satisfied?"

"Well, I can't see anything!"

"Look over there!"
So, I crossed to another window and I could see the lights of Frome quite clearly. I asked him why they kept the windows closed. He said, "Because of other people outside. They would see the ring of light. Sometimes we use them, but more often than not we don't. We do not wish to be seen. If we wish to be seen, that is the easiest way."

"Well, I have heard them described as coloured lights."

"Oh dear, yes. We come to another problem Your aircraft have what you call navigation lights."

"Yes."

"Well, you must realise we have something similar. It is a system that cannot be improved on: three major colours of any spectrum, no matter where you are or what world you come from."

"So, it is the same?"

"The spectrum is the same in any world: ours, yours."

"I can't quite understand the similarities."

"Do we not look alike?"

"Not exactly."

"Do your Asiatics look like you?"

"Point taken."

"Thank you. You don't have to come from another planet to look different. You have them right in your own world, so how much different am I?"

"Not a lot, except for your lips."
"Yes. We do have lips but they are inverted. We do have people on your world who have had bodily restructuring and have had their lips reversed. Now if my lips were reversed, wouldn't I look just like you?"

"Well, your eyes...."

"Again, shall we say your Asian continent has many people who have the same shape of eyes?"

"Yes. Well, do you have any hair?"

"Hair? Ah, you've never seen, have you?"

"Yes, I have seen you with your hood off; it looked like fair hair, but is it hair?"

So, he pulled off his hood and came over and said, "Look and feel."

And it was just hair. Fine, but just hair. I asked him if it grew. He looked at the girl and she whipped off her hood and she had long, fair hair. I said, "So everybody has fair hair?"

"No, no! We have people just like you; we have people with what you call red hair; we have hair just like you. So why are we different?"

"Were you always on your world?"

"It took a long time for that question to come! No, we colonised our world many, many millenniums ago. Millions of years in your time. Our ancestors escaped from a world and colonised that world and we are the descendants of those people."

"What world did you come from?"

"You live on it! That is why we are trying to help, because we look on you as our brothers and sisters. You will also escape from this world one day."

"Me?"

He said, "I didn't mean you personally. Your people will escape from this world one day because they will have to. There will be nothing left for them here to survive. Your scientists even today are working on that theory."

"How do you know they are working on that theory?"

"Of course, they are. They are trying to find planets capable of sustaining life and they will find many, but they will not have to go so far."

"How far?"

"Our galaxy, your galaxy, has many, many planets capable of sustaining life. They are not stars; they are planets."

"What's the difference?"

He smiled, and said, "You find it hard to believe there can be other worlds that are capable of being lived on?"

"Yes."

"Why?"

"Our scientists and astronomers have tried for long enough."

"Yes, and they have made many mistakes. They have looked too far. They have not looked at the obvious: their own galaxy; they have looked beyond it or they have looked too nearby. We know about your intended exploration of the moon. You will be successful and they will get a very big surprise to find that they will not be alone. At that point there is no doubt that we will have to do some talking on the matter, because we will not give it up."

"That's not your world, the moon?"

"No, no. It is a base. Ask yourself a question. You have had space probes circling the moon, taking pictures. Have you seen photographs of the other side of the moon?"

"I don't really know."
"No, you have not, because they cannot. It has been blocked."

I said, "So your bases are the other side of the moon?"

"No. You keep putting words into my mouth. No, I didn't say that. We have bases all over the moon. We use it as, you would call, a 'stepping stone', and we will not give it up and we will use peaceful means to keep it."

"This is amazing. We are looking at the moon every day and we can't see anything."

"I will correct you. Your astronomers have seen pin-points of light coming from the craters of the moon. Some of our mistakes. If the moon was dead, why should your astronomers see lights in the craters of the moon?"

"So therefore, you must have bases in the craters?"

"Can you tell me a better place to have bases than a readymade base? They are deep, very deep, so therefore we don't have to use so much time and energy. Our bases are underneath the surface of the moon. When we open them, obviously light will be emitted and we do know that your scientists have reports of lights coming from the craters. They admit that. Nobody will be able to come there and make war with us because you have not reached that stage yet. You will be able to send human beings to the moon but they will not be able to live in the environment and they will not be able to stay long in the environment and they will only see one part of the moon. I will explain that to you: suppose you lived on my world and you had perfected a space craft to travel to another world and you chose the one we are on here and you took off and landed in the middle of one of your huge deserts. Suppose you had to wear all sorts of apparatus for gravity and breathing purposes and you were limited with what time you had, so you were there a few hours, a day or two of your time and then returned home. What would you report? That you had seen nothing but sand and desolation."
"Yes, I get that point."

"So, therefore, there are only certain landing places on the moon that your craft will be able to come to; we have already foreseen that possibility and they are clear. There are no bases near there. We also know the limitations that your people will have when they get there; they are not our limitations because we create our own gravity wherever we are. We have special boots. We don't have any on this craft, but we have special boots. It would appear to someone who was just looking at them that they had a geometric design on the sole and heel of the boot; they create whatever gravity we require."

They use these boots to go to other planets. They go to other worlds. He said that if you looked at the pattern it would look like a geometric design but it is part of the mechanism of the boot. He said, "On the moon we have to regain gravity because there is none, so they hold us but we can reverse it. There are other worlds that we go to where the opposite is the case." He added, "Some people on your world already have knowledge of that design but they have attached the wrong meaning to it and think it is an emblem."

At that point, the other two men joined us. They could not understand the English language; they could understand other languages but not English. He explained that he was interested in finding out more about the planet. I said, "If you have been coming here all this length of time, surely you know everything?"

"Your people have lived on this planet for thousands of years and you do not know everything. We keep discovering things. You asked me earlier, did we have bases here? I did not answer you fully. Now I will answer you because at some later date we may have something for you to do, not only on our behalf but on your own behalf, so I will tell you now. We have bases in your lochs in Scotland: two lochs. We have bases under your ground; we have bases in the sea. All round your world, everywhere. You are very curious so we will show you. He showed me on the screen an area in Scotland which I am very well acquainted with, I was born there: Inverness. Then he showed me Yorkshire, which he said was one of the best-liked areas to go to. It was Todmorden, Burnley and Rawtenstall. Then he showed me Wales, then Wiltshire. He showed them on the screen, all lit up, and each was a perfect triangle.

Mike: *Did he say why Yorkshire was a favourite area?*

Yes, because of the lack of population. Also, Wiltshire. Also because of being on the ley lines.

He said, "We must follow our energy lines. If you follow them on a map you will find that they continually pass over your generating stations for generating power, especially electricity. We do need that kind of power, just to get us started. We have reserves, but we do not use our reserves unless we really have to because sources of power are available to us, so we keep that reserve in case we need it on our travels outside your world."

I was very curious about one of the men who had come in because he took no part in the proceedings, just sat and stared at me all the time. Nothing was said by me to him. Suddenly he got up and walked out and I heard him clicking just outside the door. Then the girl came in again, took a chair from the wall, sat down quite near me and started talking to my friend in their language. He wanted to know the main difference between their females and ours. I said, "I don't think there is much from what I can see."

He said, "What do you mean, 'what you can see'?"

"Well, she is wearing the same uniform as you are, very tight fitting, so obviously she is a lady. She has longer hair and quite feminine features."

"Do you find her, in your words, attractive?"

"No."
"Why not?"

"Well: a) the eyes and b) the mouth. I find it quite difficult to look at her and say she is all female, with no lips."

"But with lips she would pass as one of your females?"

"Yes. I would imagine so."

"We do have many on your world who pass as females. As I have told you before, with our technology we are very good at restructuring features. It is not a problem. The only difference is that our lips are inverted. If your lips were inverted, your mouth would be the same as mine or the young lady's."

He called her 'young lady', which struck me again as quite weird. I could not understand how they could have such a perfect knowledge of our English ways. He must have penetrated my mind because he said, "I know exactly what you are thinking: that I understand everything that you are saying and you cannot understand why. I have come to your world many times. For a number of those years, I lived on your world, before the poisons got as bad as they are. I worked on your world, as many of our people are now today. And others from other worlds."

"You keep telling me about other worlds; how many are there?"

"That's one question I will not answer. I will tell you there are many - many. All sustaining life in one form or another. Some would be beyond your comprehension; some you would understand. Some are backward by your standards; some are in advance of you."

"So, you are not the most advanced intelligence?"

"No. We are just one of many."

"Are we talking about this one galaxy?"
"No. There is life in our galaxy in many forms on different worlds but there are also life-forms outside our galaxy and one day they will be coming to your world but they will not bring anything good with them; it will all be bad. In our

galaxy everything is stable, as long as your world is stable. If we upset our world it would affect your world; you upset your world and it will upset our world, because the galaxy is intertwined with each other."

"Were you ever part of our world?"

"Never, but we had ancestors who originally came from your world. What is going to happen to your world has already happened before in another guise."
He spoke about how they had been studying our world for hundreds of years and that they could live for five hundred years.

I asked, "How old are you?"

"About half-way."

"You're over two hundred years old?"

"Yes."

"Do you ever grow old?"

"No. If you mean outwardly, no. We just reach a point when the organs fail to function. There is nothing that we have discovered that can prolong that. It just stops."

"So, you die the same as us?"

"Yes. We die exactly the same as you, because basically the life form is in all of us and, one day, that life form leaves."

"So, there is something after death?"

"Your body is a vessel that is used for a period. You are continually trying to confuse me by asking questions different to those we are talking about, but I will try and correct that by asking you this: any craft that you have in your world, whether on water, land or in the air, are you able to tell the life expectancy or usefulness of that vehicle?"

"In a way, yes."

"But it all fails at one time or another?"

"Yes."
"So does the body. The body is only a vessel; it carries a life form"

"Do you know what happens to that life form once it leaves the body?"

"It has got to find another vessel. Usually that is a very young person who has just died because the life form does not want that vessel, or a new born babe. That is not the only cause of children being born dead, but it is a main cause. Your life expectancy is improving on your world but you still have not caught up with the life expectancy that you had two thousand years ago."

"Did people live longer then? I thought civilisation was only a couple of thousand years old?"

"No. Civilisation is many, many thousands of years old. It keeps coming and going. You have destroyed yourselves and this world on many occasions and you are heading again to do just the same thing, but this time with help."

"From these Controllers?"

"There are two different races of them."

He pointed out that the Controllers had been working for many, many years in this country; that they penetrated people's minds and controlled them. He said, "You will see it if you study reports in your journals and newspapers. You will find things happening and you will wonder why but the person that did that thing did not do it voluntarily; he was made to do it. You have people in power on your world who are controlled, which is one reason why, in the very near future, there will be wars everywhere, all over your world. Senseless wars, where people are looking on and saying to themselves: 'Why? It is stupid! What is to be gained?' It is all engineered. The Controllers are turning people's minds. We cannot reverse that process; we are not allowed to by the laws of our own galaxy. We can just try to prevent it happening.

The country that you are living in, within the next twenty-five years, is going to experience times they will fail to understand, where the masses will be controlled by the few. It all amounts to three things: greed, power and wealth, but to the evil ones there is one more important thing - control."

"Why can't you control?"

"We can control, but we have laws in our universe, our galaxy. That is why we do not have wars as you have, because we obey the laws implicitly. It is reasonable for us to try and prevent the Controllers by any means but once they have succeeded, our laws prevent us from interfering; we just stand and watch. If it was not for our 'policing', things would escalate much faster than they are doing. We are losing."

"But I thought your technology was so far in advance?"

"Our technology is so far in advance that if we started anything at all that you would call warfare, not only would we destroy them, we would destroy ourselves, we would destroy the galaxy. We cannot use the resources that we have, the same as you have reached a stage now where you dare not use the resources that you have and even the Controllers try and prevent the use of them. Why do you think you have all these wars across your world yet there is control of atomic weapons, control of nuclear energy? Why does somebody not want to use just one tiny one of these weapons? Because then there would be triggered more destruction.

Under the laws of our galaxy, the Controllers cannot use these processes to further their own ends. They can use peaceful processes but they cannot use weaponry. They can only use control. If they use weaponry, we can use weaponry, and if that ever happened, the galaxy would be destroyed. They know it. We know it - and a lot of your people know it too, which is one reason why they do not use them.

The danger is that you have so much of this nuclear energy stored up which is indestructible for many thousands of years. It has to be kept very carefully; it is very unstable. Also, you have diseases which will emanate from the production of these nuclear weapons and nuclear energy. Your country and many other countries will suffer because of it. It will create diseases; it will escalate disease."

"Are we talking about cancer?"

"That is one of many. Cancer takes many forms. We have kept our eyes on the situation and what we are afraid of is that various countries on your world have reached an agreement that one country will store the nuclear waste which comes from energy. We are sure that decision has already been reached."

"You are not talking about my country, are you?"

"A part of your country is to be used. The least populated area. Unfortunately, the methods of storing it are such as to be completely unstable. There is no one-hundred per cent safe way of storing anything which creates radiation because radiation penetrates anything eventually, no matter how thick or strong it is. So, you are poisoning your own atmosphere. You are also destroying your ozone layer around your world and that is allowing in more radiation from outside your world. I don't think I have to tell you how serious that problem is. Your waters are rising. We have noted this over the years. Your seas are rising; they are claiming back what originally belonged to them. You have a major fault on your planet, the central section of which is in the Atlantic Ocean. It is getting weaker and weaker; eventually that must drift apart. If that drifts apart it simply means the sea will go."

I said jokingly, "Well, it will put out the fire!"

"What do you mean?"

"Well, everyone knows the earth is just a huge, molten ball!"

"No. It has not got a red-hot centre as you describe it. It may surprise you to know that the Controllers have bases many, many miles below your world. They can live there; we cannot."

"So, they have a different atmosphere to you?"

"Oh yes, very different. We can walk your world for a few hours without wearing any protective masks, but because your atmosphere is poisoned, we can only last for a few hours, then we must wear masks, but they must continually wear helmets and breathing apparatus of some kind."

"But you already told me that they are living on this world."

"Yes. I have told you of bodily restructuring. What we can do, they can do. May I ask you a question? How many times in your life time have you looked at a friend you have known for many years and thought: 'how he has changed!'?"

"Often."

"Do you understand what I am trying to tell you?"

"Yes."

"Your people change, our people change. The Controllers change. Your people change character, nature, behaviour. We don't change character or nature or behaviour, but we can change structurally. You can change structurally; you have doctors doing it now: creating new faces, new limbs. Very childish. Have you ever met, what you would call, an amputee?"

"Strangely enough, yes. I have a friend who lost both legs."

"He's still alive?"

"Oh yes. He walks, plays football, runs, goes swimming."

"Does he ever complain about his legs?"

"Yes. He often complains of gout. The pain is very real."

"The life force is still there. Part of your body may have gone but your life force retains the shape so, therefore, it is quite feasible that someone who has lost an arm, leg or even a finger, should feel pain in that missing part of the body because it still has the life force there."

"Yes, but can we go back to those others because you say they are controlling people. Would I know these people?"

"Your people in power, not only in this country but all over your world, make promises that they are going to do so much good when, in actual fact, they know they are going to do so much evil. They get power with the help of the Controllers, who show them the way to power and to wealth and in return they control their actions and their minds. I think we discussed earlier about brain power, where you use only a tiny fraction of what your brain is capable of. The Controllers rejuvenate the brains of the people they want to control and they allow them to use sections they had forgotten to use. "
It went on in this vein for some time and then I said, "Is it ever going to get right?"

"Yes, it is going to get right but it will take a long time."
"Don't you know?"

"Oh yes. Our learned people have worked it out very accurately. I can tell you now that it will from the year 1999, the seventh month of that year, things will start to change. There will be a series of major catastrophes because you have opted out of obeying the laws of nature. Many people will die. Things will get worse before they start to improve. Your people in power are already preparing for it."

"But nobody knows this!"

"Certain people do know but, again, we are going back to the 'greed, power and wealth' syndrome. They are already taking out 'insurance'. They have their plans made to escape the holocaust, because that is what it is going to be, a holocaust."

"Where will this holocaust be?"

"It will be on the American continent but it will affect the world because you will all get the backlash."

"So, the greatest damage will be on the American continent?"

"No, not the greatest damage. The greatest damage will be in the other countries, oddly enough, although the catastrophe will start there. I cannot tell you what it is."

"Because you don't know?"

"My friend, I do know but for your sake I will not tell you. It is better not to know. In any case, I do not think you have any cause to worry."

"Why?"

"Because when we first met, if you remember, we examined you."

"Not a very good one!"

"That's your opinion! But...I... well, let's say that you will not be here for that holocaust."

"Are you trying to tell me that you know when I am going to die?"

"Approximately."

"Is it soon?"

"I will not discuss that matter any further. You have a God."

"Is there a God?"
"Is there a God? That's quite a question! We call our deity the Supreme Being. We do have Supreme Beings."

"In our galaxy?"

"No, outside our galaxy. They are the Masters of the Universe."

"You've seen them?"

"No. We have never been allowed to travel that far."

"So, it is far?"

"Yes, but they are there. They are the intelligences who control the Universe as we know it and as you know it. At any given moment they can destroy what they have created, because they have created everything, us included."

"You told me once that your ancestors came from our world."

"Correct. Again, it was a holocaust but we were ready for it and we escaped, a select few; just as a select few will escape your coming holocaust because they have been warned and are ready for it. The thing that I find difficult to understand is that you now, at this moment, have the technology to stop this disaster and yet no one appears to be doing anything."

"Why don't you interfere?"

"Because we cannot. I have already explained to you, we have to obey the laws of our galaxy and Universe. We have laws; you have laws. The Controllers are engineering all this trouble and strife you are having on your world, which will become worse and worse because no one is able to stand up and defy them. Even the ordinary person's mind is being affected. I can explain that a bit more fully if you wish."

"Please."

"At the beginning of this century, if there had been the troubles then that you have now, there would have been public unrest, you would have had people revolting and fighting. In an advanced age, why are you not doing that now? Why are you allowing yourselves to be treated so wrongly?"

"That's a good question!"

"Because you have not got the will; your will has been destroyed. Also, as the years go on from now, your mind will become duller and duller and duller because your atmosphere is becoming more and more polluted and you are breathing in poisons which are dulling your senses and your mind."

"So that is not engineered?"

"Partly it is engineered but mainly you have caused that yourselves. You are destroying yourselves. We have talked enough. Will you eat with us?"

So, I did, and we had a similar meal to the one we had previously. The drink was the same; they didn't seem to have anything else. I started to ask questions but he told me they do not talk while they eat. We ate for 15 to 20 minutes. The drink had a tremendous effect on me.

Chapter 6
Power and Control

After the meal he suggested that we go outside for a walk, just he and I. I agreed to this. We left the craft and walked down towards the quarry. As you know, there is a dirt track which goes right around. We came down and, to my surprise, I saw about half a dozen lights flashing in the quarry. At first, I thought kids must be playing there but he said, "Don't let it alarm you, it is just some of our old friends."

"What are they looking for?"

"They are just looking. I would ignore them."

"Where do your friends come from? Where is their craft? They're not all in this one we have just left."

"No. There are three other craft. You see, we never come alone. We usually come in three or five."

"That makes four!"

"Yes, there are four here. There is one not far away. You'll see it arrive later on. I promise you that."

"I would like to see it arrive."

"You will, I promise."

We walked towards the quarry. Then suddenly, for no apparent reason, he turned around and said, "We must go back now!" So, we went back up again. This must have taken about twenty minutes or so. We went back on board the craft. He asked me to sit down again and then said,

"Have you thought over what I suggested; would you like to come back with us? If you wish, you can come back with us in February."
I said, "No."

"All right, but will you do something for me and the good of my people?"

"If I can, yes."

"Good. Just a minute."

He walked out and one of the two women came in. By the way - you know about 'Velcro'? it was just like that: she took her suit off; she just seemed to open it. She could not speak English. He came in behind her and said to me," We would like to take some of your seed back with us."

I realised then what they were suggesting. It was the second time. Well, I am a normal man but there was no way that anything like that would cross my mind. I was in a strange environment with strange people. I didn't know what to expect. I just couldn't. He seemed to understand that very fully and spoke to her and she just went out again.

He sat down and laughed. "You don't feel you can carry it out?"

"No."

"I understand. Perhaps some other time - but we have not got much time left so you must ask me questions and I'll try and answer them."

"You said to me earlier on that the Controllers were working amongst the people on this world?"

"Yes, in their hundreds, if not thousands."
"Well, how can they do any harm, these strangers in a strange environment?"

"The point is that they are not strangers in a strange environment. They have been trained from birth to take on this role. They have been bodily restructured. They will pass as an everyday human. They think like a human, they act like a human but they have more powers than a human, therefore to get into positions of authority and power is quite simple for them, very simple indeed. Power, greed and wealth are the three things that this world seems to worship above all else, so therefore these Controllers are given the wealth. They rely on the greed of humans and they rely on humans' need for power but they use it to their own ends.

They are able to control minds, whether intellectual or just ordinary people; they can control minds, they can control actions and they are doing it now, in every corner of your planet. You have people in your government who are, in truth, from another world. You also have them in other countries. We have people on your world to try to counteract the bad that has been done but unfortunately, under our own laws, the laws of our galaxy, we cannot interfere much; it is up to humans to protect themselves. But how can they protect themselves when they do not know what they are up against?"

"Well, you've confused me a little; if you've got so much power, have they more power than you?"

"No. I would say that we are the all-powerful ones but under the laws of our galaxy we cannot interfere too much in the functioning of another world. We are just not allowed to. We can sometimes nudge somebody in the right direction: somebody who is trying to find a cure for a certain disease, making some electrical equipment - we can help them, we just nudge them in the right direction because we can also control minds, but we only do that for the good of the people. In February, if you keep your appointment with us, I will actually give you the names of those in your own country who are in positions of power and who are controlled by the evil ones or who are Controllers themselves."

"If they just landed here, they would be suspect right away; they can't just walk into governments!"

"You have not listened very carefully! These people have been here for many, many, many years. They have fitted themselves into the society of this world and are now a part of it. They think like human beings, they act like human beings but their powers are beyond comprehension. Now, I promise that if you keep your appointment with us when we come back, I will give you a great deal of information."

"But you haven't given me that much up to now."

"What would you like to know?"

"One of the things worrying me more than anything else is all this talk about atomic energy and atomic bombs."

"Why does it worry you?"

"Because during the war I was in the Royal Air Force and dropped many bombs and saw the effect that they had. Three weeks after the Americans dropped the bombs on Hiroshima and Nagasaki, we were taken to see what happened. We were also shown a mock-up of the bomb. It was so small to have destroyed an enormous city; it was unbelievable."

"Yes, that is one of the dangers and you are getting more and more sophisticated. Your scientists are taking more and more risks and gambles; they are taking more shortcuts now but the one thing, up to now, they have not realised is that the waste produced from these materials will never ever lose its dangerous potential. There will be no place to get rid of that waste. In years to come, it begins in the first year of the last decade of your century, things will happen and you will say to yourself: "He told me this!" Think of what we told you and when events unfold you will realise, we knew it was going to happen. It has all been planned; it has all been organised; nothing has been done in a hurry.

In the last decade you will find that the situation will escalate. Now we intend to make ourselves known in that decade and the only way we can do that successfully will be to come in thousands of our craft and blacken your skies, it is the only way. We have attempted communication but the communications, for some reason, have been diverted. Your top people know who we are and what we are trying to do but for reasons of their own are not telling the multitude of humans; they are keeping it very, very carefully to themselves. This we cannot understand.

I promise you, when you come to that final decade of the century things are going to start working up towards the climax, as we told you before. This country that you are now in, called Britain, will become the centre for the world's radioactive waste. Your politicians, your government officials, will all have had their minds controlled by the evil ones and directed by the Controllers. Your wealthy people, by that time, will have become even more wealthy and the poor much poorer. All this is definitely going to come to pass and is all part of a plan, an organised plan. Would you step outside the craft for a few moments?"

We went out. I am still not sure what happened next but he said, "Don't look, turn round!" I turned to face the craft we had just left and as he said, "Whatever happens, don't turn round!" there was a blinding flash. No noise, just a blinding flash.

Then he said: "It's all right now, you can turn round."

I turned and I'm still not sure about this, but there were many people gathered in the centre of the quarry below. The quarry floor was clear of rock and rubble but the area was covered with a moving mass. Bearing in mind that it was night, it was hard to distinguish whether they were humans or what. He saw the look on my face and he said, "The less you see at the moment, the better. We will go back inside the craft." We went back inside.

I asked him, "How many of your craft are here now?"

"Twelve."

"Earlier you told me four and one other were coming."

"That one has not arrived yet. I promised and I will let you see it, but some more have arrived."

"Why so many here?"

"Because we are leaving this world and won't be back until February. We will all go and keep our rendezvous with our parent ship. We have half an hour of your time before we leave, so if there are any questions you had better think of them now."

"Why can't you tell me some of the names of these people in power now?"

"No. I have to ask permission first. It will be granted, but I do have to ask first."

"Why all the secrecy?"

"There is nothing secret about it. It is just that we obey the laws of the galaxy; as you obey the laws of your world; we obey the laws of the galaxy. I will ask permission first and I will be granted it and I will tell you. What use you can make of it I don't know. We have tried to tell people in authority all about us, but we find these people have all had their minds controlled. We cannot blame the Controllers for all of this because the Controllers have planned this for many, many years and your minds, as each generation grew up, became increasingly duller and duller, so each succeeding generation was not as aware spiritually as the previous one and it will keep on progressing like that. From what I know about you, I know you will think about that and realise how right it is. As each generation grows, so their mentality is not as sharp and their spiritual awareness is diminished. That is partly because you are polluting your own atmosphere but also because of the control of the evil ones. Now my friend, I must go."

We went back outside the craft and he put his hand on my shoulder and said, "I hope that you will keep that appointment with us."

At that time, I fully intended to and I said, "Well, yes, I definitely can, but you still promised I would see one of those craft coming."

"You will in... Now!"

I looked around and could see nothing.

"Look, right above you!"

I looked up and there was this huge thing hovering.

"Where did that come from?"

"Isn't that a good question!"

"But you're not going to tell me!"

"No. I will tell you some time in the future. Now you realise that we do not mean any harm. Tell your friends this: tell that when they see us not to get frightened and run away. We come as friends who want to help but we cannot help you unless you help yourselves. Again, we are complying with the laws of our galaxy."

"Were you telling the truth when you said you were from our galaxy?"

"Yes. You are part of the Milky Way and so are we."

"Now, where did you get the expression the 'Milky Way'?"

"Your people have used it for centuries. When you study a language, you study the ways of the people who speak that language.
When we do meet, if we meet, I will ask you again if you will come back with us."

"Why do you keep asking me to come back? From what I was told and what I've heard, you just grab people!"

"No, we do not! Never! Anyone who comes with us comes of their own free will. The Controllers grab - and there are many thousands of unexplained disappearances on your world that are easily explained."

"What do they take people for?"

"Sometimes to use for experimentation. Other times they are restructured and taken back to work for the Controllers. Sometimes they are just used as you use servants, in other words: slaves. This has been going on for centuries. It is nothing new."

"And you can't interfere with that either?"

"No. I have told you time and time again, we have complex laws which we must adhere to. The Controllers have enough power to create a war in which the galaxy would be destroyed completely. Even you now, on your world, have reached the stage where wars should be out of the question because if one person starts to use the weapons you have at your disposal there would be retaliation and it will not take the complete supply you have to wipe out your world."

"Do you know how many we have?"

"Yes. We know how many. We know how many the world has: about a hundred times more than enough to destroy your world."

"Really?"

"Yes. We never cease to be amazed at the ignorance and stupidity of your people. You stock-pile these weapons and you do not realise that you are stock-piling your own doom. Ten to fifteen of your missiles would be enough to destroy the world and you have literally thousands of them! One little accident....."

"Talking of accidents, you said something about the gravitational pull of the earth being altered, therefore altering the shape of the earth?"

"Yes, that is correct."

"Well, is this likely to happen?"

"Not in your lifetime."

"Well, how many years?"

"Our people have computed that it will take at least a thousand years."

"Then what is going to happen?"

"A very large chunk of your world will be torn into space, sending your world rocketing, destroying everything."

"Is this going to happen?"

"Oh yes. It is going to happen. It must happen. Come into the craft again for a minute."

We went back inside and he said, "Is there anything you would like to see before we leave?"

I had been thinking I would like to see the Control Room again and wondered for the second time if he could read my mind. I said, "I'd like to see the control place again."

So, we went up. Two people sat there. I don't know if they ever left that place. I never saw them anywhere else other than there. There was something similar to a television screen that was set into the side of the craft and it was green. These two people seemed to be transfixed watching this, they did not even look at me. He said to me, "Have you noticed something?"

"Not really. I don't even know where the controls are!"

"Watch the screen carefully." I watched it. He said, "Well?"

"It's just green."

"Cannot you see the colour dimming very slightly?"

"It's imperceptible."

"It is dimming slightly. When the screen goes black then turns white, we have to take off. That is our signal. I suggest that we leave the craft now. I will walk with you and show you where to stand to watch us take off."

We walked to the edge of the quarry. At the back end of the quarry is a gradient going down and then it flattens out. He said, "Walk towards the top as far as you can and wait there. Just keep looking at the craft." I went and stood there.

The craft started spinning, just at the top. It stopped spinning and the minute it stopped spinning it shot straight up; no sparks, no sign of any flames or anything and the only noise was a kind of 'aaah'. I watched it. The most amazing thing is that it disappeared before I could blink my eyes. It just went straight up. I felt drained and sat down. I sat there for a few minutes and I did not even feel cold. Then it dawned on me; where were the others? I never even saw them taking off; they had all gone while we were talking!

I got up and walked down the dirt track towards the end of the quarry. Something made me look to the side and there was a craft, swooping down! It was wavering from side to side, sort of waggling, then it shot straight up and away. Whether it was the same craft, I don't know. It seemed to me as though somebody had said to me: "Look here, now!" because I looked straight at it.

I went home. This was just before midnight. I went in and sat down. My trousers were soaking wet. My wife asked if

I wanted a cup of tea. I said I would make some coffee and got up. She cried, "Where the hell have you been? Look at the settee!" It was soaking wet!

When I took my clothes off to go to bed, my whole body was tingling; the skin seemed to be crawling. It is quite a difficult sensation to explain. My whole body was like that all night long.

Next morning, I was curious, I went back to the quarry with my son, Mike. Although he had heard of these things, he did not know my story. I never told him; he was only twelve at the time. I wanted to see if there was anything in the centre of the quarry where I had seen this huge, moving mass. There was nothing. Nothing was disturbed. We walked up the dirt track to where this craft had been most of the time and I looked for a sign of where it had been. There was hard snow and frost and not a mark anywhere. So that craft never touched the ground.

Chapter 7
Aftermath

About four weeks after my experience the doorbell rang. My wife answered it. She came back and asked me to deal with them, thinking it was Mormons. I went out. There were two men who I immediately took to be Mormons, to be quite honest. They were very smartly dressed in dark suits and one man said to me, "You will forget your experiences."

I said, "What are you talking about?"

"A piece of advice: forget everything you have been told, everything you have seen."

"Are you Mormons?"

"Just remember what we said."

They turned round. We had a long garden which led to a dead end, you could not go anywhere. There was a path going onto the road. The car park for the five houses was just there. There were no buses. I went in, then the penny seemed to drop and I ran out. I was going to ask them who the hell they were. I ran down the path; it is downhill. I looked. No one there. Not a soul. That happened twice.

The second time they came it was exactly the same situation. I was upstairs having a bath. My wife came and said there were men at the door who wanted to speak with me. I pulled on a pair of trousers and went down. It was two different men but dressed like the first pair. One of them said, "Don't talk to the press; deny everything."

I said, "Who are you, please?"

"Don't talk to the press and deny everything."
Again, that happened. This time I went down to the garden gate and watched them walking along the lane. I let them go down the three steps onto the road and then I ran to see what kind of car they had. Nothing! They had gone! No car, nothing! That worried me.

That same afternoon three reporters turned up: two men and a woman. They were from the *News of the World*. Norman Ray was the editor at the time, I believe. One man said, "We want to talk to you about your experiences."

"What experiences?"

He said, "Oh, come on! It's worth a bit to you!"

I said, "I've no idea what you are talking about."

"You landed up in hospital the first time, didn't you?"

"Where are you getting all this information from?"

"We have ways of getting our information."

"Well, nothing happened!"

"Come on! You were taken to hospital and you were pretty badly mauled about and you were also suffering from very severe burns, most unusual burns; they were spotted burns! What happened to you? Is it anything to do with the Warminster flap?"

"I have no idea what you are talking about."

I don't know where they got their information from. The only thing I could think of afterwards was that one of the nurses, doctors or one of the staff from the hospital had telephoned them, because the *Western Gazette* printed a small bit about a man being found with his clothes ripped, and how the police were looking upon it as a bit of a mystery.

Then about six or seven weeks afterwards, again two men came. In all they came seven times. Each time they were a different pair.

Mike: *What colour did they wear?*

Dark grey. Very dark grey

All of them?

Always dark grey.

Did they have short hair?

They all wore caps. Everything looked brand new.

Did the clothes fit in with the period of fashion?

Oh yes. Very smart.

Did you see any cars with them at all?

No. None.

Did they have any rings or watches on?

None. No rings; no jewellery. I don't know about watches but no rings. They were not outright threatening; they didn't say much, but what they said and the way they said it was more than enough. Bearing in mind what I have been told about bodily restructuring and these people being in positions of power, I have my own theory. These people look like very successful businessmen. They looked as if they had been poured into their clothes. They didn't look out of place in those clothes. They looked as though they were made for the clothes and the clothes were made for them.

When they spoke, did they display any expression on their faces?

Not at all. That is the thing I didn't like. They didn't threaten me in so many words, but they did frighten me, I must admit.

OK. Please continue.

By this time my nerves were really frayed. I had written to the Air Ministry and the Ministry of Defence. I wrote to the Prime Minister. I received no reply from any source, not even an acknowledgement. I was becoming, I think, a nervous wreck. My kids told me recently how different I became then. I was quite a patient, tolerant father, but I was turning on the kids and the wife for every little thing. This went on for about three months altogether.

One night I came home and my wife said, "Sit down1 What is wrong? Tell me now!"

"What's wrong? What do you mean, what's bloody wrong?"

"Don't speak to me like that! Just tell me what is wrong. Let's talk about it."

I said nothing. It was only a week until my February appointment with them but by this time I had built up a kind of fear. I did not know what to do. About four days before I was supposed to go back to the quarry my wife and I had a row. A bad one. I packed my stuff and went to London.

I went to see a solicitor in London the following day and had the house, everything I had, transferred to her. I changed my name, not legally, but it is still changed now, and I went on the road. I landed in France with exactly fifteen bob (shillings). I did not know where I was going to go, yet that night I spent in a hotel. I had a lovely dinner and wine and ended up the following day with fifty francs! I washed dishes and cleaned tables at the hotel and got paid for it. I thought: "This is easy!"

So, I moved on and did very well - picking grapes, etc. I went to Bonn, then I got a job for two weeks on an Italian cruise ship which goes down the Rhine. I moved on to Switzerland, Italy. I began to enjoy my life but I was not sleeping. I kept having vivid dreams that they were coming for me, looking for me.

There are gaps in this story because it is difficult to remember everything in sequence, but one of the things that comes into my mind is very important. In one of the conversations, he told me that if it was not for them, the world would have been destroyed many years ago. They protected it from destruction. Another thing he told me, which impressed me and scared me when I was travelling, was that "Wherever you are, if we want to, we can find you!" I could not understand how I had been so friendly and easy-going with them.

Mike: *Did he say how they could find you?*

Yes. In the first talk we had. We were talking about the human brain when he said we had lost the power of using the majority of the brain. We only used a tiny fraction. "You have forgotten how to use it! You do not even try! And that is how we can find you. We can find any individual because your brain is like a receiver and transmitter. It emits signals and we can track any person down by that."

93

That's why I kept moving. It's childish, I know, but I kept moving all these years. I travelled around.

There then followed a conversation between George and the UFO investigators about the sightings then current in Bonnybridge, Scotland. George's niece lived in Scotland and had seen a UFO at close quarters.

George continued:

When my niece from Bonnybridge[8] contacted me, I was so excited. I flung some clothes on, flung some clothes in a case, jumped in the car and raced up to Scotland! My niece, who was always a sceptic, now very much believes. She saw a craft. It landed near her but she heard a howl and ran away. This reminds me of when I was warned not to approach the craft when it had first landed. Perhaps she was warned off. I have an irresistible urge to go back up there and nothing will stop me. I only came here to keep my promise to you.

One of my biggest mistakes was in not going back and meeting them again. When we shook hands, he embraced me, just like a human being does.

I have never met the Controllers but he told me what to watch for: they have no nails. They have nails but you can spot that they are not real straight away because they have a very bluish tinge where the cuticle is and they cannot disguise that or do anything about it.

He told me, "If you ever meet them, the Controllers, it will be to your disadvantage, but greedy people fall into their clutches."

We got to the last meeting, the third meeting, which lasted around three and a half hours, and we had a walk outside the craft, talking, then we came back into the craft. When we were back inside, he said, "Listen carefully. Events are going to happen that will have a direct effect upon the whole planet, leading to a catastrophe in early 2000 which will be manmade. The minds of the majority of people will be affected by the leaders of the various countries. These leaders, in turn, are going to be controlled. The thoughts of the majority of people will not count; every time they object to a decision being made it will be over-ridden by the few. These people will make themselves wealthy and very powerful. This island of Great Britain is going to be the focal point. It will take some years, but as you get to the last decade of this century you will find the whole thing will start to escalate. You will have bloodshed, you will have tears, not just in one part of your world but in every section. Brother will kill brother. Son will kill mother and will not even think twice about doing so. They will all be controlled by the few, who in turn will be controlled themselves.

By the end of the century, you will have exhausted a lot of your natural resources and you will have weakened the structure of your planet so much that there is a danger of part of your planet being torn off and floating away into space.

I have already shown you pictures of what the inside of your world looks like. Now I will show you some more, taken recently. You have destroyed the infrastructure of your planet and unless this is stopped your planet could wobble off its axis. If it does that it can destroy the whole galaxy and this is the reason why we have been trying to do something to help. We have people amongst you who are trying very hard to right the situation but, unfortunately, you also have the Controllers who are manipulating people in power.

You are a normal person. You have trusted us and we are trusting you. If you can contact agencies on your world who will defy these people in authority, it may help, but I am personally afraid that it is an impossible task because your leaders will not listen to you. They will be so obsessed with their power and their wealth and greed. In other words, the power and the wealth will be very unevenly distributed amongst a very few.

But, in the last decade of your century there will be an alteration which, again, cannot be avoided, that is going to entail disease which is uncontrollable and which cannot be cured; there will never be a cure. Your cancers will become incurable. You will bring on yourselves diseases which cannot be cured. By the end of the century, you will almost have destroyed yourselves although you will not be aware of that until some little time later. Many of the people on your planet at that time will have no mind of their own; they will not be able to control anything they do or say. They will survive, just.

In the meantime, we have already made arrangements and plans to get as many as we can off your world when the escalation gets beyond control."

He said that we are going to have diseases that we have never heard of and they will be incurable. He said there will be major disasters all over the world. Those in power will be destroying the atmosphere deliberately. The people in charge have been chosen carefully and are being controlled.

He said, "Don't doubt for one second. They do not even know themselves they are being controlled because their greed for money and power over-rides everything else, so they are quite prepared to go along with it. In the last decade matters will escalate at a tremendous speed. Your whole ecology is going to be threatened and virtually destroyed. So, by the time the major catastrophe happens in the new century there will be literally billions of people who will already be dying from diseases. Those who are not dying from diseases will be getting killed by their own friends and relations. People will destroy each other with a smile on their faces. Only a handful will remain. That handful will roam around with their minds gone. They will continue to kill each other. Those that we take off your planet will never know about it because we will never tell them what has happened to those left behind."

George added: He said the disease had been introduced into this world. That it had nothing to do with the sexes although the sexes will be blamed for it. They told me this twenty-eight years ago. He said, "If they knew the cause they would know the cure." He told me that he was going to give me more information in February, once he had asked permission. He said I would know when they were coming back.

We talked for another half hour or so and just had a normal conversation. He just wanted to know if I had ever had an operation; asked me about my life, etc. He told then it was time to leave. I wondered why they always had to leave suddenly. He explained they had to rendezvous with other craft, then return to their planet. I was quite 'put out' because I liked him and he obviously liked me.

He walked with me about halfway along the quarry track then, again suddenly stopped and looked up at the sky. He said, "I must go now. If you want to see us leave, just go into the clearing and look up." Well, I did. The craft came over the top of the quarry and as it did, it waggled. Then it just shot off. It went straight up. I saw it for about three or four seconds, but then it just seemed to disappear.

I stood there for quite a while, looking all round to see if I could see anything. It was a very clear night but it just disappeared. I walked back down to my car. He had told me that when they are approaching this planet, they turn on their side, which makes them almost impossible to detect to the naked eye. I thought this might have happened.

The biggest mistake I ever made in my life was in not keeping that fourth appointment in the February.

Mike: *You said earlier, he wanted to know about any operations; what else did he say?*

It was just a conversation; just like talking to you. He did tell me I was going to live a long life and that I would retain my faculties. I thought about that last year in Liverpool, when I went to the hospital for an examination after a slight heart attack. They gave me a thorough examination and I'll never forget what the doctor told me: that my internal organs are twenty years younger than my years. I am 79.

Do you think it might have anything to do with the drink they gave you?

I don't know. I don't like to imagine things. I am a realist. I wasn't conscious all of the time on the first visit. I kept coming to and then going again. There are no marks on my body which would suggest any kind of an operation, if that is what you are getting at.

Did they ever talk to you about implants?

No.

Did he mention a breeding programme?

Yes. He said they have many sons and daughters here, interbreeding. He said that the Controllers have a bigger breeding programme.

Did he say how this was done?

Not exactly. He said, "If the child was to be born in their image it would be destroyed. When a man and woman mate, the percentage is higher for the child to have the mother's characteristics. The chances are that three out of every ten children born to the Controllers and their mates would be perfectly normal to outward eyes. The others will be malformed. Bodily restructuring would come into that programme, but there will be a percentage that will have to be destroyed before they are born." I asked him if they then monitor the progress. He said, "Oh yes." He told me that there is many a man walking the planet who adores his son or daughter, not knowing the child is not his and that not even the mother knows that. I don't understand what he means, but that is what he said.

Did he comment if the Controllers were using an earth woman who was carrying a child which needed restructuring, when that child would be restructured?

No. He did say, "You have many people who disappear from your world and who are never seen again; hundreds of thousands. A percentage of those people will be in that quota. Sometimes it is safer for the evil ones to do that. We had to do that, but now it has been stopped because we do not wish to harm, so if we find the breeding programme has gone wrong, we induce a miscarriage or an abortion. That is so simple for us to do.

Did they ever mention about animal mutilations?

Yes. That's the Controllers. Around Warminster there were some mutilations of animals reported. I asked if they had done it. He said that the evil ones had been experimenting to see if they could form any kind of human life from animals.

People should think about what is happening. They still say it didn't happen in Warminster. Slates fell off roofs, windows smashed, dogs howled, hens stopped laying, cats with their hair on end, cows stopped giving milk - and nothing happened! Hundreds of people saw them! During one night the whole area was sealed off, including with tanks. On the Sunday black limousines arrived, apparently from London - and nothing happened!

Two public meetings were held in Warminster Assembly Room in the summer of 1965 to discuss the constant sightings of craft in the sky and so many people turned up, including journalists and media crews that over 350 were turned away from the doors - and they still say officially that nothing happened!

He told me it would be the leaders who would cause all this, so who can we complain to? I thought I would be listened to. I gave my rank and number; I have medals. I thought they would listen to me. There was complete silence. They just don't want to know.

[8] Bonnybridge had a spate of UFO activity in the 1990s.
http://www.streenge.com/places/bonnybridge.html

Addenda.

As with many of such tales, discrepancies can be found. For instance, at the start of his story George remarks that the aliens he met had no fingernails. At the end he says he was warned that the Controllers had no finger nails. Does this mean that both races have no fingernails; that he actually met the evil ones or that he simply got muddled with the passing of time?

The overall picture painted of control and catastrophe can be seen and felt more readily in today's society. However, predictions given to him do not seem to have come to pass, or not in such a dramatic way as implied. Again, most such predictions and prophesies fail - maybe that is because they are predictions of possibilities should things continue as they are going. However, life involves random events and actions, unforeseen events and decisions, all of which change the tide of affairs.

What has not come across on these pages is the emotion of George as he told his story. The number of times taping had to be stopped or sessions abandoned because he broke down in despair at how his life had been changed by his encounters or in fear at the predictions given him or with sorrow for his family and what he did to them by leaving or with regret at missing his chance to go back and hear more. Sometimes, as he talked, his voice would lift and his face break into a grin and he would exclaim: "Oh, I had forgotten this until now!" as the act of remembering opened up more memories.

In the end, you have to decide for yourself. Anything can be believed whole heartedly or have so many holes picked in it that it disintegrates to dust, depending on your own viewpoint and attitude. Whether this tale is born of actual experience or fertile imagination, it echoes things reported by many, many thousands of humans across this planet.

Something is going on: either a phenomenon of collective consciousness and imagination, collective paranoia, exploitation of the general populace by a powerful, secret section of humanity or real interaction between our species and at least one other. The biggest favour you can do yourself is to read all you can on these matters and decide for yourself.

Whatever the true nature of reality and our place in it; one thing seems clear: that we always have a choice between darkness and light. That Love or Light is a real energy force and that if we open ourselves to that energy and concentrate on things that feed our spirit, our choices will be right ones.

Books by Mike Oram

Does it Rain in Other Dimensions?
ISBN: 978 1 84694 054 5

The Zen of Ben
ISBN: 979-8676856670

The Strange World of Jimmy Hayes
ISBN: 978 1 907710 17 9

Coming Soon: The Further Adventures of Jimmy Hayes

Books by Fran Pickering

The Weird and Wonderful Cook Book
ISBN: 978 1 907710629

The Weird and Wonderful Fun Food Book
ISBN: 978 1 907710643

A Simple Home Guide to Colour Therapy
ISBN: 978 1 907710599

Printed in Great Britain
by Amazon

84141160R00068